EARLY REVIEWS FOR CURATIVE CULTURE

★ ★ ★ ★ ★

"It's rare that one finds a book so enjoyable to read, and, at the same time, so instructive on important matters in life... my only disappointment was that it had to come to an end!" –Mateen

★ ★ ★ ★ ★

"A great read that challenged me."–John

★ ★ ★ ★ ★

"'Culture reveals the proof of what we really believe.' That statement alone is worth the price of the book."– Russ

★ ★ ★ ★ ★

"The book is filled with practical insights and real-world examples that make the concepts feel achievable, not just aspirational. This isn't a fluffy, feel-good book. It's a wellresearched, thoughtfully constructed guide for leaders who are serious about creating a workplace where people can thrive." – David

★ ★ ★ ★ ★

"Doug's wisdom could not have come at a better time." – Scott

★ ★ ★ ★ ★

"I've accepted Doug Shaw's challenge for my company. A lot of people talk (a) good game about workplace culture, Douglas Shaw has lived it." – Roy

★ ★ ★ ★ ★

"HUMANITY AT WORK: Applause to Doug Shaw - Must read!" – Amazon customer

★ ★ ★ ★ ★

Could there really be a practical antidote to the cynicism and burnout that so many of us have come to accept as normal? I'm happy to report that this book is a resounding "yes." – David

★ ★ ★ ★ ★

"A must-read for leaders who want to shape culture with courage and care." – Bill

★ ★ ★ ★ ★

"I just finished Curative Culture by Douglas Shaw, and it gave me ALL the good vibes about what work could be. I love that this book highlights creating workplaces that actively nurture, restore, and build well-being." – Shellie

CURATIVE CULTURE

STEPPING AWAY FROM A TOXIC WORKPLACE

—— LEADERSHIP EDITION ——

Douglas K. Shaw

Curative Culture | Stepping Away from a Toxic Workplace
© 2025 by Douglas K. Shaw

Published in the United States by Cedar River Media, LLC.
www.cedarrivermedia.com
ISBN (Paperback) 979-8-9986788-0-6
ISBN (Hardcover) 979-8-9986788-2-0
ISBN (Ebook) 979-8-9986788-1-3
ISBN (Audiobook) 979-8-9986788-3-7

For information, address Cedar River Media
inquiry@cedarrivermedia.com

**CEDAR
RIVER**
MEDIA

TABLE OF CONTENTS

ACKNOWLEDGEMENTS

I would like to acknowledge Tim Owen posthumously since I just learned of his passing, and his wife, Edie, who together served as my pastors, mentors, and friends in early life. They helped to direct me into an education that dramatically changed and shaped me. Tim also served as a reference for my first career position out of graduate school, which elevated me from a cow town to the national and international stage.

Tom Robbins, Ron Short, Warren Prigge, and Chris Derrick all befriended me at varying points in my life when true friends were few. While they didn't know each other, they all shared similar qualities of character, collegiality, and intelligence, which they liberally shared with me. Life would not be the same without them.

To those who trust me enough to join and work in and on my company, I owe a debt that can never be repaid. John Donne was right, "No man is an island, entire of itself . . . a part of the main." In a way, this book is a love letter to you in which I attempt to describe the work community we share. You are all truly a part of what is right with the world!

This book and the others that have come before would not have been possible or cohesive without the encouragement, structure, and candor offered by my writing coach and editor, Meredith Siler. Special thanks to my daughter, Laura Cheezum, for her patience and diligence in editing the copy for this book.

And lastly, out of reverence, I wish to thank my family. To my parents, who have gone ahead, your love and sacrifices will never be taken for granted. You are treasured in my heart until I can, again, stand beside you. My sisters, Pam and Lori, who are the only living records bearing witness that my childhood tales are true because you traveled the same path, bear the same scars, and emerged to a better life as a part of the American Dream. And to my sister Mary, who was lost along the way, may you now know the love hidden deep within my heart. To my cherished children, Laura and Graham, I have marveled as I have watched you grow, mature, and face the harsh winds this life has to offer. I take solace in your love and devotion to your own families and pray that this family-owned business provides shelter from the storm. And to my dearest Kathryn, who always has my heart and my back, thank you for choosing me. Your constant love and devotion are amazing gifts that bring insight and delight wrapped in the intelligent curiosity and tenderness you offer every day, even in the creation of this book. Thank you for so generously sharing your life and your family with me. I choose you!

PREFACE

As we know, toxic work cultures tear people down, demoralize them, and leave a lasting negative imprint on the human spirit. They can leave individuals doubting themselves and questioning their self-worth, and if not treated, the toxicity can permanently damage people or even further spread the disease.

We have all known people who have been caught in an environment that has battered them to the point of tremendous frustration and demoralization. Who hasn't heard someone say, "You don't want to work over there. That place is toxic!" Sadly, it may have even been our own personal experience.

"Toxic" is an almost universal word to describe things we want to flee from or avoid at all costs. It can be a plastic bottle of something we found under the sink or out in the garage, something we've stepped in that's stuck to our shoe, a classmate in school or a professor, a relative, an "ex" or a long-time negative relationship, or, for our purposes, a poisonous corporate culture.

But there's another, perhaps more important, aspect of toxicity. It is important because of its insidious nature. You and I, as leaders, might not even be aware of the toxicity that we, ourselves, are creating or allowing. Because of its prevalence in the marketplace, toxicity may be all we have ever experienced, and therefore, we've recreated this soul-singeing environment in our own business or nonprofit organization without even realizing it.

There must be some reason you're reading this book right now. Perhaps you're just curious and, in your lifelong learning, want to increase your awareness. It's also possible you "smell" something funny in your company and wonder if it is worth investigating. And maybe, just maybe, you know something is definitely wrong in your company or organization, and you feel compelled to act.

It's my privilege to be the founder and CEO of a 30-year-old company that employs scores of highly talented women and men. The ideas they bring to strategy meetings are transformed into words and images that move millions of people to make decisions about giving hundreds of millions of dollars to our clients' charitable causes every year. But my journey began with my first career position, where I worked in the headquarters of an international organization employing thousands of people worldwide. I was on the receiving end of toxic leadership and found myself wondering if it was me. Was I simply not getting it? Everyone around me was frustrated and talking about it, but no one seemed to be able to do anything.

My supervisor certainly knew there were serious

leadership issues emanating from the CEO's office. He was in the very undesirable position of clearly seeing the leader's shortcomings, yet he was unable to impact change. This was and is a great organization with a very noble mission, yet it seemed that any real accomplishments were made almost despite the toxic culture at headquarters.

Even though I had advanced in responsibility and opportunity, I began seeking positions elsewhere. I just couldn't see my way out of having to work around the CEO to accomplish anything of import. What surprised me was the ability of my supervisors and peers to continue to live in the swirling chaos. A few years later, the entire headquarters staff informed the board of directors that either the CEO would have to leave, or they would. The board finally listened.

I had moved on by this time, but for the next 12 years, I found myself in companies with other significant culture issues. Partners preyed upon each other, using their employees as chess pieces to accomplish their ends. As a Vice President, I found myself continually pitted against my peers, with the expectation that this would propel us to perform at higher levels in the pursuit of greater profitability. In actuality, it catalyzed high employee turnover, declining profits, and broken relationships.

In my last position as an employee—Senior Vice President in a direct response fundraising agency, I realized that in order to experience the kind of corporate culture I envisioned, I would have to create it by starting my own company.

In all my roles up to this point, I became driven to understand the dysfunction around me and my own role as a participant. For most of my career, I had been a consultant to hundreds of companies, large and small, across North America. Through this lens, I had the vantage point of being counsel to and an observer of corporate cultures. What I witnessed may come as no surprise to you. Employees or coworkers do not set the tone for their corporate culture. They certainly participate in it, but they have little or no impact in creating or changing it on a corporate scale. This can only be done by the highest level of leadership.

Another significant influence on my thinking about corporate culture was exposure to the lives and teachings of women and men of great distinction and character. Max De Pree, who was the chairman and CEO of the Fortune 25 Office Furniture Company, Herman Miller, and Dr. David Allan Hubbard, the 3rd President of Fuller Seminary, a world-class scholar who served in this role for over 30 years, both contributed greatly to my view of leadership and the use of power in the workplace.

While I studied at Fuller Seminary, I encountered Dr. Roberta Hestenes, the first woman to be a tenured professor there. She became the Board Chair of the great Christian humanitarian organization, World Vision International. Dr. Hestenes went on to become the 7th President of Eastern University near Philadelphia, serving in this capacity for nine years. Hestenes, both in her writings and class time, greatly inspired my view of women in leadership.

Others mentored me through their writings. Robert K. Greenleaf, an executive at AT&T, went on to lecture at MIT, Harvard Business School, Dartmouth College, and the University of Virginia. His book, *Servant Leadership, A Journey into the Nature of Legitimate Power & Greatness,* impacted my thinking about the benefits of the serving nature of leadership.

So, in October of 1994, I stepped out of my role as an employee and took the risks associated with becoming an employer. But what kind of corporate culture would I create? Which leadership model would win out? The tumultuous or the temperate? If toxicity was the norm, was it possible to create an alternative?

It's worth pointing out here that while we all have heard or experienced the word toxic, we don't seem to have a one-word descriptor for what we would consider *great corporate culture!*

Perhaps less familiar to us is to hear a friend or colleague say, "I wouldn't trade where I work for anything! I feel valued for who I really am!"

So, while searching for a one-word antonym, the descriptor that appeared to be most appropriate out of an extensive list was "curative." What drew me to this choice was that it seems to suggest a process of recovery or getting over something poisonous or toxic. The most applicable definition, though, is simply "serving to cure or heal." The etymology of this word, curative, is from the Latin curare, which means to watch over, attend, treat (sick persons), and restore to health.[1]

Let me be clear in my use of this word when describing a corporate culture. I am NOT intending to suggest that it is the responsibility of ownership or leadership to become "healers" or therapists. Rather, by employing this word/concept, I intend to show there is a hopeful alternative to the life-draining aspects of the workplace. It's accomplished through watching over, attending to, and restoring the health of the work experience for both employer and employee. What I'm suggesting here isn't going to seem practical; I'm fully aware of this, but let me quickly add, creating a curative culture works. **I know, I've done it.** A bold statement, I realize, but by adopting the qualities of a curative culture, our 30-year-old company has an employee retention rate averaging 9.5 years, as compared to the national median of 3.9.[2] What may seem counterintuitive or even countercultural

---

[1] "Curative," in *Merriam-Webster Dictionary*, n.d, https://www.merriam-webster.com/dictionary/curative.

[2] U.S. Bureau of Labor Statistics and U.S. Department of Labor's Chief Evaluation Office, "EMPLOYEE TENURE IN 2024."

is the establishment of curative culture has not negatively impacted profitability. In fact, as this cultural planting has taken hold, our profitability has increased exponentially.

Often, inexperienced, inattentive, or callous leadership is at the root of a toxic work culture. This, sadly, may often be more prevalent than most of us realize and, therefore, experienced by many. If this is true, then it is likely that a great number of us are looking for a place to work that might help us recover from our past toxic experiences and hence be in search of a company that is "curative" in nature both for the leader and the follower.

It's also possible that you've been tasked with turning around an organization with toxic tendencies. Hopefully you find some insights on the following pages useful.

The phrase curative culture may conjure up any number of images. Perhaps it may be of service to envision a work situation with **thriving corporate health**: a work environment created to allow a work community to feel safe, think, and do its best to make the world a better place while having hope for growth and career advancement. Distractions and drama are intentionally held to a minimum while encouraging quality thinking and productive action. Profitability or, for not-for-profits, abundant funding, is positively influenced by this sense of well-being.

This book is *about the nature of a curative work situation, what it looks like, and the positive ways people can relate to each other while working.* It's about people looking forward to engaging with their colleagues, so much so that they do not want to miss out on what happened when they were on vacation. It's about intentionally creating a work community that people do not want to leave once they decide to join. And, if they are somehow lured away, they can't wait to return. Can such a place exist? If so, how is it built? Can it be maintained? It's my hope that you will find the reading of this book thought-provoking and well worth the investment of your time.

For the sake of clarity, I've intentionally chosen to define my terms throughout the book. As a result, you'll see dictionary definitions liberally employed. I've done this because I believe words matter. Word choices reflect the values we embrace. For example, I've chosen to use the phrase "work community" rather than "job" or "place of employment." You will also see that I frequently use the word "coworkers" rather than "employees." This choice emphasizes the collaboration and interdependence of leaders and followers or employers and employees.

As I've mentioned, I know what I'm proposing is countercultural. Stepping away from toxic workplaces requires us to think and act differently as we guide those who look to us for leadership. You may also find yourself wondering what my references to the wonders of nature have to do with creating corporate culture. They serve to shift the way we think away from the urban confines of steel, glass, and concrete, open our minds beyond the view from our office windows, and help us experience the world in a way that may feel foreign to many of us today. I intend to provide a perspective of what most of humankind experienced long before our recent generations came on the scene.

There are many still living who were born in the 1940s and 50s, decades when much of our language began moving away from the use of nature in our metaphors, to those born since the 1980s, whose imagery is more closely associated with technology. A quick example is "nature's library," as in "Each tree in the forest is like a book from nature's library",[3] vs. "Google it!" While many used to marvel at the wonders of nature, today, it is, perhaps, more common to marvel at what is available on our iPhones, Apple Watches,

[3] Jason Downs, "25 Metaphors for Nature," *Idiom Insider* (blog), November 27, 2024, https://idiominsider.com/metaphors-for-nature/.

and Smart Rings. What follows is not a diatribe against technology; I personally embrace and use it daily. Rather, it is a clarion call to consider or reconsider the valuable life lessons in the natural world that have existed since the very beginning.

For most of my work life, I traveled by air, an incredible statement were it to be heard by most of the people who have ever walked the earth. The first scheduled passenger airline service only began in the U.S. on January 1, 1914.[4] By the time I stepped away from my consultant role, I had logged almost 2.5 million miles on American Airlines alone, not to mention all the other carriers I'd used. I only tell you this because I can vividly remember looking out the window at 38,000 feet, watching the earth below with its mountains, forests, and rivers passing below me at 540 miles per hour. I felt trapped inside a metal tube passing over people's farms, ranches, small towns, suburbs, and cities. I envied those who

---

[4] "The Early History of Commercial Air Travel," Aviation Oil Outlet, n.d., https://aviationoiloutlet.com/blog/early-history-commercial-air-travel/?srsltid=AfmBOopga GgBUHoFYvSYAl9NKnpkASHmBDLAX6ZsfxuqzeywqtX56If3.

had lived and worked in the same community for their entire lives. I knew the names of flight attendants, limousine drivers, and hotel concierges. Those down below knew each other.

I began to feel the call of the earth upon me with such power that I knew I needed to reacquaint myself with the sounds of rushing water, the smell of rain and cedar trees, and the feel of a dirt path under me. Things didn't change overnight, but I did begin an intentional journey of re-acquaintance with the rural experiences of my youth. When I finally arrived, I found nature there, just being itself, scooting over to make room for me.

There is so much wisdom to be found in nature, which, in my belief system, I prefer to call Creation. There is order and intentionality in the universe, and I seek to remind us of how reverence for nature impacts how we relate to the people and world around us. When we look to step away from toxic workplaces, the purifying sights and sounds of nature can breathe new life into the way we view work communities both inside and outside the windows of our offices or workspaces.

As a corporate leader, you carry an incredible responsibility to generate profit for your company. Nonprofit leaders also carry their own burdens. They bear the weight of generating adequate funding for the causes they herald. None of this can be accomplished without the participation of the people who follow your leadership. The concept of a curative culture places an intensely high value on those *people* who share your vision, mission, and values, as well as the questions they bring into the workplace daily.

In many ways, this book assumes you have already worked through your vision and mission. Numerous others have written to help you with these aspects of your leadership. While vision, mission, and values are an inseparable leadership trio, in this book, we will focus on the belief that culture is primarily shaped by *values*. For this reason, in the following pages, we will focus heavily on the attributes of a highly functioning, curative work community.

Lastly, you'll quickly see that I value the power of storytelling. This ancient art form has proven its value by remaining in our minds long after other thoughts have escaped us. Stories are also a means to convey our humanity, a benefit when asking, as I am, for us to remove the walls between our work and our value as people.

DOUG SHAW

January 2025

I
THE CULTURE WE CREATE

I happen to have been born in Washington State. Most residents and visitors agree that its natural beauty speaks to the soul in magnificent ways. At sunset, the shining white volcanic peaks turn the color of the peaches and plums that grow in abundance in the dry heat of Central Washington.

But it's called "The Evergreen State" for good reason. Washington is home to 25 species of conifers.[5] Among them are Douglas fir, western red cedar, Sitka spruce, Ponderosa pine, and Pacific yew, with the most abundant being the Pacific silver fir. Having access to these treasures of nature is a privilege.

I clearly remember the day my wife, Kathryn, and I were touring Reid Harbor in the San Juan Islands near the

[5] WA Forest Protection Association. "Trees of Washington State – Washington Forest Protection Association," September 4, 2023. https://www.wfpa.org/forest-facts/trees-of-washington-state/.

U.S. - Canadian boundary waters in the Salish Sea (the vast inland water system that includes Puget Sound). We were moving almost silently along the harbor's shore in our little 10-foot inflatable dinghy, marveling at the emerald-green water's ability to light up with diamond-bright reflections of the sun. I'm quite certain the cool salt air was the purest I had ever had the privilege to inhale. I could both smell and taste it as though it were a "new world" fountain. And all along the shore, for miles, there were glorious palisades of evergreen trees. In this moment, the grandeur of the Creator's palette engulfed me. As overcome as I was, I could still make out the words of heaven being whispered into my ear, "And to think, not one person on Earth can create even one needle, on one branch, on one tree." In this transformational moment, my feelings of insignificance were strong but welcome; it was instructional, not hurtful. They led me to give voice to the ancient songs of wonder and joy at the unexpected creative expressions of the Significant One, the Creator who had only to speak, and it was so. Yes, there are so many life lessons in nature, but only if we are willing to place ourselves downwind to pick up the soft chords and quiet choruses around us. Perhaps this was in the thinking of Joyce Kilmer when he wrote:

Trees[6]
I think I shall never see
A poem lovely as a tree.

A tree whose hungry mouth is prest
Against the earth's sweet flowing breast.

A tree that looks at God all day,
And lifts her leafy arms to pray;

A tree that may in Summer wear
A nest of robins in her hair;

Upon whose bosom snow has lain;
Who intimately lives with rain.

---

[6] Harriet Monroe, ed., *Poetry, a Magazine of Verse*, vol. 2, 1913.

Poems are made by fools like me,
But only God can make a tree.

Unlike nature, we know corporate culture *can* and *is* created by us. In fact, it seems *it will be created* just by our very existence. It feels somewhat inescapable, much like the old saying, "Wherever you go, there you are!" Similar, perhaps, to walking on a pristine sandy beach, eyes fixed on what lies ahead. But once you glance backward, your footprints are there, to be seen by anyone who travels the same sandy stretch. It's your shoe tread, in your shoe size, spaced according to your stride. We all leave our mark as we travel through life.

If, by our very presence, we change our environment, then it seems that each person who joins a work community likely makes their own impression; the community is impacted in some unique way just by their presence.

It's intriguing to think that organizations are the sum of the varying personalities who work in them.

Coworkers are naturally curious and constantly engaged in conversations about...their coworkers. What it's like to work alongside, work for, or manage others occupies much of any company's coffee conversations. How often have we heard a coworker ask, "What's she like?" when inquiring about a new colleague's personality? It's a question more related to the person's behavior, communication style, competence, and character than her preferences. Some of what's really being asked is, "Will I like her?" "Can I trust her and her intentions?" "Is she worthy of my respect?" "Will we work well together?" "Is she safe?"

If coworkers continually talk about their coworkers, one can only assume they talk about their supervisors, too. While their positions vary, the questions about supervisors are largely the same as those about coworkers, "Do I like them?" "Can I trust them and their intentions?" "Are they worthy of my respect?" "Do we work well together?" "Am I safe?" What would any caring leader give to be able to answer "Yes" to all their coworkers' questions?

Just as the beauty of nature is an expression of the creative attributes of the Almighty, it might be said that people are, too. Theological tomes have been written in the hope of better understanding *imago Dei*, the doctrine that teaches mankind is made in the image of God. The implications of this teaching are myriad and extensive. For our purposes, let's simply assume that all people are created by God to reflect his image. Allowing this influences how we relate to our coworkers. Each and every one of us in the work community has inherent value.

If, as human beings, we reflect God's image, then perhaps it's best understood when we say we all have the capacity to seek wisdom, faithfulness, goodness, justice, mercy, grace, and love. These are not common workplace words. But they are common needs that we share, and when we acknowledge these attributes in ourselves and our employees, perhaps we begin to see people differently.

One year, during the COVID-19 epidemic, when just about everyone was trying to isolate and work from home, my son Graham and I decided to deliver bonuses to my leadership team. It required the better part of the day, but with careful route planning and proper notification, we found the whole experience highly inspiring and enlightening. About 10 to 15 minutes before our arrival, I called each team member to ensure they were home and prepared to meet us at their front door. I saw a different side of each person we visited as we pulled into their driveways. I saw them at their homes, outside of the context of the office. I could see their houses, their yards, their neighborhoods, and the smiles on their faces as they opened their front doors. I could tell they were moved that Graham and I would take the time to hand-deliver personal notes and bonuses to them. It was a day that left my son and I full of appreciation for the good people we have leading my company. It made a very positive impact on them, too; they knew that we saw them as people as well as employees.

There is, however, an inherent risk of accepting the perspective offered by embracing *imago Dei*. If we believe all people are created in the image of God, it calls us to embrace the belief that all people have intrinsic value established by their essential nature.[7] In other words, not only do all of our employees and coworkers have value, but they have a divine imprint on them by the Creator himself! On the face of it, the risk may not be fully evident. Just plumb the depths of this dark stream for a few feet, and some rather unsavory possibilities begin to bubble to the surface. We might find ourselves asking, "Is it really possible to apply this thinking to my workplace?" The very thought that *imago Dei* might

---

[7] Colin Brown, *The New International Dictionary of New Testament Theology* (Zondervan Publishing Company, 1975).

apply to the more unsavory of our coworkers might cause us to pause or even recoil. There is no assumption here that, in embracing *imago Dei*, everyone will always be their best selves. Unfortunately, we are all flawed and cannot aspire to perfection or sometimes even likeability. But the question remains: is it worth the risk to care about *who* people are, as well as *what they can do* for my company?

If we desire to believe the axiom, "no risk, no reward" this may be a more than adequate test of our sincerity. Is it actually possible to desire success for those we like or respect the least?

Several years ago, I found myself in an agitated state with one of my employees. It wasn't the first time, either. In fact, many of my interactions with this person left me muttering and vowing to dismiss this employee at the next available opportunity. I wasn't alone in my frustration. Several other members of my leadership team and staff were growing weary of the negative headwind this person brought to the workplace. One day, in a meeting with my COO and HR, I declared my intention to terminate this employee when we next met. I could see my colleague's empathy for my position, but I also heard their concern for the impact that outright dismissal would have on this person and our company. He was, after all, close to retirement age and very well thought of in our industry. They decided to ask me if I wanted this person to succeed. And the truth was, I no longer did.

During the ensuing week, I found myself feeling regretful about my decision to terminate this person who, at his age, would likely find it very difficult to find another position. I also knew he was the sole breadwinner in his household since his spouse had a life-threatening physical condition, which also meant they were depending upon the insurance benefits offered through employment. I also had a nagging feeling that I wasn't living up to my own values. By no longer wanting this person to succeed at his job, I had abandoned my desired behavior of treating this person with dignity.

During my next meeting with my COO and HR, you can imagine their surprise when I said, "I simply cannot bring myself to fire him." I saw their jaws drop quickly, followed by a smile of relief on their faces. As we talked, they expressed support for my decision. They knew I was headed toward an action that wasn't in keeping with the values Douglas Shaw & Associates espoused. I decided to offer the person in question a few weeks of sabbatical to decide if he wanted to work here at the company since his behavior had indicated frustration with me and the way the company was being run. Upon returning from sabbatical, he was to declare either acceptance of my leadership and a modified work assignment or his decision to terminate affably with severance. To my own surprise, during our next meeting, which included HR,

I found that I wanted this person to take the modified work assignment and the continuance of the health benefits his family so desperately needed. In fact, I was taken aback when, during the meeting, he declined both the sabbatical and the modified work assignment. What I didn't know until that meeting was that he, too, was struggling with deteriorating health, and his workplace behavior was heavily affected by the physical pain he was bearing. He knew he couldn't continue employment, so he resigned effective immediately.

At this point, I must acknowledge that what I have just described is foreign thinking in most places of business. The employee in question would have likely been shown the door long before our protracted meetings. What I'm describing is a fundamentally countercultural way of thinking about workplace culture. Is it more time-consuming to lead in this way? Absolutely. Is it a profitable investment to make in people? Absolutely! In no way does actively caring about your employees as people threaten profitability; rather, I have seen it enhance performance, employee tenure, and the bottom line.

There is no question that the culture I'm proposing we create will require a very different way of thinking about people. But there is, after all, a reason why you decided to read this book. Perhaps the reward is found in a navigable course to the likeability, trustworthiness, respectability, collaboration, intentionality, and well-being that we all seek in our own lives and for our purposes here, in our own workplace culture.

Perhaps more companies would benefit from knowing there does not need to be a high wall between what we believe about people as human beings and how we behave toward people in the workplace.

2
THE CULTURE WE INTEND

Accepting the belief that corporate culture can be created and that we impact it by our presence within a work community begs the question, "What is the nature of the culture we intend?"

To be intentional in creating culture, we would do well to make a distinction between culture and vision, mission and values. While vision and mission are most certainly driven by intention, they are the *reason* or *purpose* for an organization or company to exist. They guide us in determining *what* we do.

Culture, in our context, is the *heart*, the *feelings* of a work community's body, and culture is most closely aligned with and expressed in *corporate values*. Values are a statement of *who we want to be or become. Culture, then, reveals the proof of what we really believe.*

What a company or organization truly values and believes, it prioritizes. Coworkers have an uncanny sense of what is valued or prioritized in their workplace. They can just feel it.

For most of us, there are places we've been in our lives that can evoke feelings. East of Seattle, a massive floating bridge, several lanes wide, lies atop dark blue Lake Washington, linking Mercer Island and the Eastside to the Seattle metropolitan area and Puget Sound. When you drive eastward, the topography changes quite quickly into the emerald foothills of the impressive Cascade Mountain Range. The steep curving climb to the summit of Snoqualmie Pass is covered with a mixture of evergreen and alder, bigleaf maple, and vine maple deciduous trees, among many others.

As a small boy, I would traverse this place of rugged, heavily forested mountains with my dad in his old Chevy pickup with its familiar smells of sweat, mortar, grease, and cigarettes. We listened intently to the whine of the transmission and felt the pull of gravity upon the compression of the old truck engine. Over the years, he lost many heavily worn vehicles on this perilously narrow two-lane highway. It had steep drop-offs and deteriorating wooden snow sheds, which are wooden tunnels built to shelter the road from avalanches. The 3,000-foot climb to the summit was ominously referred to as "the Pass." So, we always held our breath until we made it to the top. Once there, we would often stop to stretch our legs and refuel, and my dad would go into the old lodge at Snoqualmie Falls to grab a cup of coffee. I would sit in the pickup, with the stern warning to "not touch anything," and look out the window. This is where I first discovered the difference between East and West.

The summit of Snoqualmie Pass has a very distinct dividing line of foliage. Right at the very top, the trees change.

Looking east, the deciduous trees give way to conifers, mostly Ponderosa pine. The sword ferns, salal, and moss of the western rainy side of the mountains become rocky, needle-covered dry forest floors on the snowy eastern side. The underbrush that makes many western Washington forests impassable gives way to lodge-pole pines, sagebrush, and high desert in what we refer to as "east of the Mountains." To this day, whenever Kathryn and I drive the multi-lane, guardrail-protected I-90 East over the Cascades, I think of the old highway and the perils of "the Pass" and wonder at the discoveries of my youth. Successfully crossing Snoqualmie Pass is a constant reminder of the many surprises of nature and the obstacles that have been overcome. Each crossing evokes feelings of something accomplished. It's a place of natural wonder that carries reminders of how difficult life used to be.

Workplaces evoke their own set of feelings, too. For some, going to work is "the grind," the uphill climb that feels unsafe because of the lack of guardrails. For others, the thought of beginning their workday elicits feelings of familiarity, purpose, accomplishment, and camaraderie. Certainly, there are many variations of feelings in between. The footprints that follow each of us into our day are woven into those of our coworkers, creating a path that helps shape our workplace into a blended set of feelings.

The intrigue of knowing we contribute to the creation of our workplace culture simply by being there is only heightened when we consider, once again, the feelings of coworkers. When they arrive at work and begin communicating with their leaders, they not only bring their own contributions to culture, but they also bring questions, and their questions never seem to change. Every day, it seems, is a new opportunity for leaders to answer, "Do I like them?" "Can I trust them?" "Are they worthy of my respect?" "Am I safe?" A leader who has intentionally chosen to be caring is able to answer "Yes" to most, if not all, of their coworkers'

questions.

3
THE CULTURE WE EMBRACE

My father was a brick mason. Some of my earliest memories of him were sitting in his lap with his strong left hand held out for my inspection. With three-year-old fingers, I would find myself tracing the deep callouses and corns that had formed upon his hardened fingers and palm. In the curiosity of childhood, I would ask, "Do they hurt?" With his right hand, he would hold his cigarette to his lips, take a deep drag, turn his head away, and blow smoke across the kitchen. Then he would quietly answer, "No, son."

He was a craftsman, highly skilled with his plumb line, level, brick hammer, and trowels. He was a builder. Like so many men of his time, he had served in the U.S. Army in the Pacific theatre of war under General Douglas MacArthur. He was 27 when he received his draft notice, quite old for a recruit, but his country had called, and he dutifully answered. During basic training at Fort Lewis, Washington, he learned the rigors of soldiering. Upon completing his training, he was loaded aboard a troop transport in Seattle and made the long sailing to Australia. He was eventually posted on the Island of Leyte in the Philippines. Like so many who fought, he seldom discussed it, and when he did speak about his experiences, he made it sound like his role was mundane and insignificant compared to that of so many others.

He was a builder, both in his generation and his trade. When the war was over, what he called "VJ Day," or Victory over Japan, he went back to his mortarboard and trowel with his brothers, who were also in the trades and went on to build much of south Seattle.

Near the end of his life, my dad would sit out in his yard at a picnic table, smoking cigarettes and drinking instant coffee. One of his five brothers, Uncle Bob, would drop by from time to time, and they would talk and exchange family news. I happened to be visiting from out of town on one of those days and joined them at the picnic table. Listening to their conversation, I heard them say, "I saw Frankie's son, Kevin, the other day," my dad said. Bob asked, "Is he still working at that office job?" "No," Dad replied, "He works for a living."

At that moment, I realized that, according to my father's work culture, I did not work for a living. Uncle Bob had just nodded in agreement when the statement was made. They had both been bricklayers who had used the strength of their bodies to "put food on the table." They were brothers both by blood and by a shared life of physical labor.

That picnic table afternoon, almost 40 years ago, has stayed with me. It was the day that I felt excluded from my father's work fraternity. My footprints had followed me to that table from my summer jobs, university, graduate school, and several years of office work. Dad and Uncle Bob's footprints led back to lives of scaffolds, long days in the sun, wind, and misty rain stacking brick and concrete block, a skilled monotony broken up only by the welcome creativity afforded by the careful shaping and placement of an occasional decorative stone project.

On several occasions during my career, I have marveled at the fact that, in our direct response fundraising company, Douglas Shaw & Associates, we get paid to think, talk, and strategize. While we certainly make our own impact on the world, we do not build anything with bricks and mortar. We deal in ideas rather than structures. Today, "working for a living" means something quite different for most people I know.

Understanding that fundraising, like most other forms of communication, is becoming more and more digital, it remains that many of our ideas would never be implemented if it weren't for the efforts of those who labor long hours in the print industry to bring them to fruition. Forklift drivers move massive rolls of paper from loading docks to printing presses, and press operators and plate makers form an army of people who ensure every fundraising letter is printed and ready for the mailing house. There, rows of imaging equipment print the names and addresses of donors onto the letters, reply slips, and envelopes. Next, workers feed letters and reply slips into finely tuned inserter machines before the stuffed envelopes are sealed, stamped, and placed into mailing trays. Once palleted, they are shipped to a third company that prepares the mailing trays for efficient delivery across North America. Long haul truckers carry them over the highways to post offices across the continent. Postal workers take over and disassemble the pallets, carrying every piece of fundraising mail to donor's mailboxes and mail slots. Here, the ideas our company has strategized, written, and designed are finally in the hands of the caring people who then must decide if they can and will give funds to help change someone's life.

The organizations and ministries we serve, our clients, are the critical link to saving and changing lives. Their calling, expertise, and commitment help people attain or regain faith, hope, and dignity. Our company has little reason to exist without them.

I hope my dad would have been pleased to know that we created a space for one of his most-used bricklaying trowels in Kathryn's favorite lighted case in our home. It's there to honor his legacy of "working for a living." This critical tool of his trade carries the patina of his last batch of mortar on its blade, and the handle is smoothed and shaped with indentations of his right hand worn into it by a lifetime of labor. I sometimes open the case, reach in, and hold his trowel in my own right hand. It reminds me that

I wouldn't be here if he hadn't been there. He labored in the heat of summer and damp chill of Northwest winters, stacking brick, block, and stone while building homes for people, and those neighborhoods still stand today.

The act of working carries a sense of worth regardless of position. Anyone who has ever suffered the indignity of being unemployed knows the feelings that come from standing on the outside, looking in at everyone else going to work.

Our subject, though, is about what happens when a person is on the inside looking out. It's about how it feels to be at work. Is it a place of fairness and goodness? Do coworkers feel valued? Is the company contributing to the betterment of society? Is it part of what is right with the world? Do the people who work there feel proud to tell their family and friends about their work? Do coworkers and their leaders respect each other? If the answer to these questions is "no," it is very likely coworkers, as my wife Kathryn has said so well, "will feel the same loss of self-worth and dignity as being unemployed."

Leaders are responsible for creating the guidelines for a culture we can embrace. They do this by forming and articulating a company's vision, mission, and values. Experience indicates that the formation of a vision and mission, although somewhat taxing, requires less energy than the formation of corporate values. This comes with little surprise since most of us find it easier to answer the question "What do you do for a living?" than "What are your corporate values?" Yet, it is still the task of the leader to establish or formulate the values that will guide the company's culture. In other words, it is easier for leaders to answer the question, "What is the purpose of your company's existence?" than, "How does it feel to work in your company?" But answer they must. Caring leaders know that just as feelings are equally as important as ideas, values are equal in their standing to vision and mission.

We all know of companies that have enjoyed great success in the creation of new products, services, or causes that were revolutionary in their ideas, and yet they failed the values test. It seldom, if ever, ends well for the company or for the people who have embraced a toxic culture. Living here in Washington State, we are keenly aware of the financial woes of The Boeing Company. At the time of writing, Kelly Ortberg, the recently installed CEO at Boeing, has publicly acknowledged that cultural problems are foundational to stabilizing this historically great company.

Caring leaders also understand the value of people, especially if they accept the premise that we are all made in the image of the Creator. This high view of all human beings will guide the hand of a caring leader as they formulate and articulate the corporate values needed to begin answering coworkers' questions about the people they work alongside, such as, "Can I trust them and their intentions?" "Do I like them?" "Are they worthy of my respect?" "Am I safe?"

How many of us grew up hearing the parental admonition, "Do as I say, not as I do!"? This was largely in response to the statement, "Well, YOU do this...". It was often a rebuke regarding undesirable behavior or language. In effect, however, it was a declaration of a double standard. It's OK to do or say these things when you're an adult but not as a child. Perhaps it might have been an attempt to have children behave better than their parents, helping them to be better people. It was not an effective course of instruction then, and it isn't now.

Caring leaders understand that formulating and articulating corporate values is not enough. These all-important statements of character require that they be embraced by leadership first, followed by coworkers. Double standards are no more convincing in a corporate setting than they were at home. When we as leaders embrace and practice the values we have formed and articulated, we communicate in the most powerful and convincing manner available to human beings.

4
THE CULTURE WE EMBODY

One of the most impactful leaders from whom I had the privilege of benefitting, both in the classroom and in his leadership of the educational institution where I took my graduate studies, was Dr. David Allan Hubbard. He was the third President of Fuller Seminary and a renowned Old Testament Scholar.

In the classroom, Dr. Hubbard transported us back to the ancient days and ways of the biblical prophets. He made sense of Hebrew texts that would have otherwise been incomprehensible to me as a relatively new theological student. A true master of his craft, he made the patriarchs knowable as human beings with their doubts, dilemmas, and the heart cries of their souls. In listening to him deliver his lectures, I could feel the wind, taste the grit of sand, and hear the cacophony of the ancient Hebrew communities, making the Old Testament more relevant than I had ever imagined. His words were poetry woven into a treasured tapestry of divine-human interaction.

However, Dr. Hubbard was also the leader of Fuller Seminary, a world-impacting institution. His influence was felt in every area of the Pasadena campus and emanated from it throughout the theological world. As a student, I could feel it, from the quality and beauty of the Oakland Avenue campus landscaping to the world-class faculty Hubbard attracted and empowered. The institution's quality was equally reflected in the precious Dead Sea Scroll fragments displayed carefully under glass in the world-class campus library.

Dr. Hubbard introduced me to a Fortune 25 leader of one of the best workplaces in the world, Max De Pree, who was the CEO of the renowned furniture-making company Herman Miller. Max De Pree was also the chairman of the board of Fuller Seminary for many years. He and Dr. Hubbard, for a time, team-taught The Institute for Christian Organizational Development (ICOD). By this time, I had graduated and was finding my way in my first career position in a nonprofit relief and development organization near Chicago. Thankfully, my employer could send me back to Pasadena for this career-shaping leadership institute.

Throughout my time at ICOD, the phrase "legitimate power" was woven into the presentations. It piqued my interest since "legitimate power" implied there was "illegitimate power" as well. But the value of the Institute content was intoxicating, and it was being delivered at such a pace that, in the moment, I didn't seek clarification; I just took notes as fast as my pen would go.

Two years later, I received an invitation to a Fuller Alumni gathering to be held near my home at the time, in Glen Ellyn, Illinois. Dr. Hubbard was the guest of honor. I was never one to attend alumni events, but this one drew me in. I couldn't wait to hear him speak again, and just maybe, I could ask him about what he meant by "legitimate power."

It was a rather heady event. The hosts had a very lovely home and had clearly made every effort to make the evening special. Fine fare was served in the best china and crystal. After a welcome to all, Dr. Hubbard was introduced. He spoke softly, commenting briefly about current happenings at the Seminary and thanked us for coming out on that chilly evening.

Once the formal part of the evening concluded, Dr. Hubbard circulated amongst those in attendance. Before I knew it, I found myself standing right next to him. He was quiet, and I was quiet. The awkwardness was killing me. How do you make small talk with Dr. David Allan Hubbard? I knew he played the clarinet, but that was a non-starter since I knew nothing about the instrument. So, I decided to go for it, "Dr. Hubbard?" "Yes?" he responded, turning toward me, "I had the privilege of attending ICOD." "Oh, good! How did you find it?" "I loved it!" I said, almost too enthusiastically. "Yes, Max and I had fun with that one," he said, smiling ahead. Max, I thought…he just referred to the CEO of one of America's greatest companies as Max. Then I asked my burning question, "Dr. Hubbard, during the institute, you and Max De Pree often referenced the phrase, "legitimate power," can you tell me what you mean by this?" "Well, you've read Greenleaf, haven't you?" he asked. He'd asked it in such an academic tone that I wanted to reply, "Oh, Greenleaf, yes, I was reading his fourth volume just the other day." But, alas, I don't consider myself an academic, and I certainly didn't think I could pull it off. It was a good thing, too, because Greenleaf had never written four volumes of anything! So, I just simply responded, "No." "Well, you need to get yourself a copy of Greenleaf's *Servant Leadership*. I believe the title is *Servant Leadership, A Journey into the Nature of Legitimate Power & Greatness,* Paulist Press[8], I think. " "Oh, thank you!" I stammered, "I'll pick one up!" Now, I was still in my early 30s and working for a faith-based nonprofit. It's probably no surprise; I didn't have a book budget.

I remember returning to work the following Monday and telling my assistant, Jeanne, that I would like to get a copy of *Servant Leadership.* She smiled and wrote it down. She knew we didn't have a book budget either, but I must have carried on some about wanting to buy it because, on my last day at that organization, Jeanne presented me with a hardcover copy signed by everyone in my department. I was moved to tears.

As for the book, I devoured it! I made notes all over it and dog-eared the pages over the years for easy use. I found it to be more of a reference book and dipped into it by chapter whenever I needed perspective on a sticky work situation.

---

[8] Robert K. Greenleaf, *Servant Leadership [25th Anniversary Edition]: A Journey into the Nature of Legitimate Power and Greatness (Paulist Press, 2002).*

This well-worn "trowel" of my trade now resides with my son Graham, who is on his leadership journey in our company. Robert K. Greenleaf is worthy of your consideration. His book, *Servant Leadership, A Journey into the Nature of Legitimate Power & Greatness[9]*, is a compilation of articles, essays, and presentations that he made during his life.

The 25th anniversary edition carries this message on the inside front cover; I couldn't have said it better, "In the quarter century since these ideas were first articulated, the notion of servant leadership has gained ever more disciples in business schools, among executives, in government and in public and private institutions. Greenleaf was among the first to analyze the qualities of leaders and followers—and the necessity for leaders to be attentive to the needs of others."[10]

After a few years of working in the nonprofit sector, I was recruited by an agency that raised money for not-for-profit organizations. This change allowed me to better provide

---

[9] Greenleaf, *Servant Leadership*.
[10] Greenleaf, *Servant Leadership*.

for my family and to help more not-for-profits utilizing direct response fundraising. As for the leadership in the new job, it was anything but "attentive to the needs of others." A few months later, I asked the company's president, "Have you ever heard of the book *Servant Leadership* by Robert Greenleaf?" He snapped his head around and, raising his voice, bellowed, "DON'T YOU EVER MENTION THAT BOOK AGAIN!" I, rather sheepishly croaked, "O-Okay…"

So, I took my copy of Greenleaf out of my office, hid it in my briefcase, and carried it home, where it remained for many years. I was now in the rough-and-tumble agency business and I wasn't about to forget it!

For the next 12 years, I kept my head down, learned, and practiced what fundraising great, Bill Sturtevant referred to as "The Artful Journey"[11] of helping people to give to causes they believed in.

It wasn't until I was 71 years old that I had the good

---

[11] William T. Sturtevant, *The Artful Journey: Cultivating and Soliciting the Major Gift*, 1997.

fortune to read Larry C. Spears's liberating words, "Our personally embracing servant-leadership does not require the approval of our supervisor, or our organization's chief executive. We don't need anyone's permission to personally do our best to act as a servant-leader. It's our choice."[12]

Even after a lifetime of commitment to the servant-as-leader concept, and at my age, it still feels good to receive Spears's permission and encouragement.

Hubbard, De Pree, and Greenleaf embodied the culture of servant leadership. I attempted to put my own feet in proximity to their footprints as I built Douglas Shaw & Associates. As with any leader, I did not have a perfect track record of always saying the right thing or behaving without regret. Just ask my coworkers; they have an uncanny sense of when I'm being true to my values. They can just feel it.

---

[12] Philip Mathew, *Finding Leo: Servant Leadership as Paradigm, Power, and Possibility* (Wipf and Stock Publishers, 2021).

5
A COMMUNITY OF SERVANT LEADERS

"My thesis, that more servants should emerge
as leaders, is not a popular one. It is much more
comfortable to go with a less demanding point
of view about what is expected of one now."[13]
— **Robert K. Greenleaf**

A curative culture can only be so if it provides a communal commitment to serving each other. The catalyst for this commitment begins with the leader who understands that their coworkers observe every action they take, every word they speak, and every wince, eye-roll, or nod of approval. Once seen, they hold each gesture up to the light to see if what they've just witnessed aligns with the professed values of the work community.

This became all the more evident to me when I recently participated in a celebration of Douglas Shaw &

---

[13] Greenleaf, *Servant Leadership, 24.*

Associates' 30th anniversary. Staff, spouses or significant others, and long-time freelance creative partners flew in from all over the country. At one point in the evening, an open microphone was made available for anyone to speak about their experience working at the company. I was both fascinated and amazed at what people chose as evidence of the authenticity of our corporate values. One person cited a meaningful 2-hour conversation with a leader that occurred almost 20 years before while sitting on the roadside awaiting highway assistance for a damaged tire. Another led us back in time to when we had our own on-site direct mail production facility, and with a deadline looming, someone discovered a serious error. They expressed how moving it was to see most of the company's top leadership hurry through production department doors in response to a company-wide page for help manually sorting 2,000 letters to high-level donors that were mistakenly out of order. It was particularly inspiring to hear what spouses had to say about the company's impact on the quality and purposes of their own lives.

When leaders become servants, something in work communities changes for good. In corporate America, Herb Kelleher (former CEO of Southwest Airlines,) Cheryl Bachelder (former CEO of Popeyes Louisiana Kitchen), Howard Schultz (former CEO of Starbucks), and Tony Hsieh (The founder of Zappos) all caused the business world to pause and consider the opportunity to think differently about work and the good that can be accomplished when the leader becomes a servant of those they lead. Some leaders who pause and consider this change how they see and relate to the human beings within their work communities, like those at Nordstrom and Balfour Beatty in the U.K. and around the world.

There are so many others in small companies and large corporations that have thought long and hard about the culture they intend to create. Thankfully, Robert K.

Greenleaf not only thought about leadership, but he, due to his relationship with the top leadership of AT&T, had a more than adequate sample size to test his ideas, beliefs, and realizations about the role of leader as servant. This led him to conceptualize and be among the first to articulate both the term and role of "servant-leader." Fortunately, his essays and talks were combined and edited into book form, which was first published in 1977. I have referenced it earlier, but it bears repeating here. The book *Servant Leadership, A Journey into the Nature of Legitimate Power & Greatness*, when it was released, "a new paradigm of management entered the boardrooms and corporate offices of America."[14]

As expressed in his book, Greenleaf's thinking is foundational in the building of a curative culture, as are the writings of Max De Pree. Ten years after Servant Leadership was published, De Pree published his own articulation of "authentic leadership" in his profoundly articulate

---

[14] Greenleaf, *Servant Leadership.*

and elegant work, *Leadership is an Art.*[15] While there are so many excellent books on leadership, there are none more thought-provoking to me in the process of creating a curative culture. Perhaps it is their emphasis on the "why" of leadership more than the "how" has attracted me to them.

Stepping away from toxic workplaces is not easily done. It requires a different way of thinking about work for both the leader and the follower. Perhaps the hardest part is believing that curative work communities exist. The countercultural nature of this work community can feel like a unicorn to most. However, once someone encounters curative culture, very few people will ever choose to return to the toxicity that led them to pursue this life-sustaining alternative.

---

[15] Max De Pree, *Leadership Is an Art* (Michigan State University Press, 1987).

6
CURATIVE CULTURE

The phrase *curative culture,* as referenced above, is defined as a culture "serving to cure or heal."[16] It helps us envision a work situation where there is a revitalizing and refreshing sense of well-being in the work community. It's an intentional work environment that *allows* community members to feel safe, think, and do their best to make the world a better place while having the hope for personal growth and career advancement.

As noted earlier, we don't have to look far to find toxic workplaces. I've shared some of my own stories where leadership, either through incompetence, personality disorders, or greed, impacted me greatly in deciding to create my own company. What I haven't shared is one of the fictional characters who helped to shape my vision for a positive, curative

---

[16] Merriam-Webster, "Curative."

culture. Charles Dickens's *A Christmas Carol*, written in 1843, has resonated with so many of us that hardly a Christmas season can pass without someone turning on the television and settling in with a warm throw and a large bowl of popcorn to relive a film version of its telling. Of all the memorable characters created by Dickens' quill, Fezziwig stands out to me. As the Ghost of Christmas Past carries Scrooge back in time to see his younger self as an employee of Fezziwig, who was dancing at the company Christmas party, even Scrooge can't help but be moved by his old masters' generosity:

"Say that his power lies in words and looks; in things so slight and insignificant that it is impossible to add and count 'em up: what then? The happiness he gives, is quite as great as if it cost a fortune."[17]

Fezziwig has something to teach us all as we consider a work experience in which coworkers have the *opportunity* to participate fully in a community where people are valued as

---

[17] The Editors of Encyclopaedia Britannica, "Fezziwig | Victorian Era, Ebenezer Scrooge, Christmas Carol," Encyclopedia Britannica, May 10, 2010, https://www.britannica.com/topic/Fezziwig.

human beings. Some aspects are worth special consideration.

First and foremost is the reality that all members of our work community are, in essence, volunteers. They are our coworkers because they choose to be. Assuming we've hired people who are highly talented or give a strong indication of becoming so, and their values fit well into the existing work community, most, if not all, members of our work community are highly marketable elsewhere, and we would be wise to remain cognizant.

A second consideration is the inevitability of disagreement, frustration, and conflict among some work community members. Just as each person brings their unique experiences, talents, and perspectives to the community, they also bring their expectations, opinions, and scars. How a community learns to negotiate these differences reaches into the very heart of a curative work culture.

Even if a leader makes a great effort to create a

curative culture, it in no way ensures that its members will *allow* the benefits of this intentionality to salve the scars they may bring with them into the community. However, if highly attuned recruiting practices are carefully employed, most coworkers will indeed allow themselves to prosper in the safety that a curative culture offers.

Unfortunately, even carefully orchestrated screening during recruitment cannot detect all of a candidate's emotional wounds. Some of us have become quite adept at subjugating the less desirable aspects of our personalities to secure something we really want. But as we know, time is the ultimate truthteller. None of us can hide who we really are in the long term.

Over time, each coworker's preferences, opinions, and points of friction become evident. How each coworker communicates and behaves, as differences occur, is a contributing factor to the feelings of safety, respect, and trust levels within the work community.

There is a high level of confidence in the field of psychology that "family of origin" plays a defining role in determining the fingerprints left on our psyche that directly impact how we respond to our social environment. An excerpt from an article published by the American Psychological Association reads,[18]

> "The family of origin and past relationships can often help us understand what is so perplexing about our current situations and why we so often seem to fall into patterns of relating to others that are not our best selves. There is much about our relational actions and choices that seems beyond our ability to comprehend and understand."[19]

It's when we are "not our best selves" that a work community's culture is tested. Attempting to decipher why friction develops between coworkers can be "perplexing" indeed. Understanding our own scars and how they influence

---

[18] "APA PsycNet," n.d., https://psycnet.apa.org/.
[19] Dean M. Busby and Emilie Iliff, "The Impact of Family of Origin Experiences," in *Routledge eBooks*, 2017, 134–43, https://doi.org/10.4324/9781315678610-14.

the footprints that follow us, as well as those of our coworkers, can perhaps be of great service when tensions arise.

A distinguishing feature of a curative culture is seen when performance issues or conflicts arise among coworkers. As cited above, prompt remediation is critical in maintaining a sense of balance within the work community. This is especially true when it comes to dysfunctional leadership.

Experience tells us that those in leadership positions quite often need self-correction. As position and power increase, it becomes more difficult to mask family of origin scars. These undesirable characteristics, together with positions of authority and the stresses of leadership, can simply be too much for a leader to constantly hold their undesirable behavior in check.

Just as followers observe promotions, they are also acutely aware of course corrections delivered to those around them, especially leaders. I have witnessed the development of a critical connection between followers and leaders when those leaders who require course correction in their own performance accept this feedback with grace and humility. Coworkers not only observe how leaders receive feedback from their supervisors, peers, and followers, but they also emulate it!

There were two highly placed leaders who worked in a company I had the privilege to serve for many years. Both leaders contributed significantly to the growth of the business, and they rose in responsibility accordingly. Each had their own distinct experience and leadership style, but what stood out most was how each handled coursecorrecting feedback from the CEO.

At first, one of the leaders, whom I'll call Linda, saw her team members as being there to "make her look good." She drove her reports hard, was sparse with praise, and seldom recommended any of them for promotion. As with most big issues, this one came to the attention of the CEO. He did his homework and then called Linda into his office to address the grievances of her team.

Linda's first response was quite defensive. She didn't deny the behaviors attributed to her; she argued that her actions and attitude toward her reports were appropriate. The CEO listened carefully but then leaned over his conference table and, looking directly into Linda's eyes, asked, "Is this how I have treated you over the years?" He asked this question with measured intensity in his voice. "Well . . . no, no, I guess not," Linda responded as she looked down at the table. The CEO decided to let the awkward quiet do its work. He just sat there, observing. Linda was clearly uncomfortable in the silence that seemed to go on interminably.

Finally, she lifted her head and eyes to meet those of the CEO. "So, I obviously need to make a change in how I perceive those who report to me?" she said as a realization more than a question. They talked for several minutes more. The CEO affirmed Linda in her role but indicated they needed to get together once a week for the next month or two to work through how she viewed leadership and followership.

On another occasion, the CEO found himself in a meeting with yet another leader, Troy. Similar issues had surfaced, and a similar conversation commenced. But something was quite different in this meeting. While both leaders had been defensive, Troy's response differed greatly from Linda's. He denied the allegations of his team and was quick to point out their weaknesses. When the CEO confronted him, Troy became very angry. The CEO shared some observations with Troy about how reports prefer to be treated and how leaders can inspire rather than punish or intimidate. With each observation, Troy defended himself. "Yes, I know this. I learned this years ago." During follow-up meetings with Troy, the CEO continued to encounter an attitude of defensiveness and anger, often hearing the phrase, "Yes, I know that." It doesn't require a high level of insight to understand how Linda surpassed Troy in her continued career growth to eventually become a trusted senior-level leader of the company where both she and Troy worked. I don't remember what happened to Troy. All I know is that I heard from one of his reports that he wasn't there anymore, and nobody knew where he went.[20]

There are at least three other actions that, when practiced, can add significantly to the sense of fairness in the community. One of these is seeking to understand both the individual(s) and the nature of the issue(s) at the core of the undesirable behavior. Here, understanding involves moving beyond identifying the issue(s) and into a greater knowledge of the *perspectives* of the individual(s) involved. Another way to say this is to gain empathy by "put-

---

[20] Douglas K. Shaw, *The Six Essentials of Rapidly Growing Nonprofits*, 2022.

ting yourself into their shoes." For many leaders, this does not come easily. It may require extensive listening to the individual(s) with minimal talking, perhaps while taking copious notes and allowing several days of living with the words, thoughts, and feelings that were expressed.

A second action that might add to the sense of fairness in the community is to take a self-inventory by asking, "Do I really want this person to succeed?" Depending upon the nature and frequency of the interpersonal friction, the answer to this question may not be an immediate "yes." Again, referring to any notes taken during the listening session can be of great service. Revisiting the precise words spoken versus our own recollections can help keep our thinking in the other person's shoes. Also, before considering further action, you might find that revisiting the work community's corporate values can clarify the situation.

A third facet contributing to the sense of fairness in

a work community involves close collaboration. It can be immensely helpful to borrow the strength of others when working through the issues surrounding individual(s) exhibiting undesirable behavior. There is great benefit in collaborating with and listening to the perspectives of trusted colleagues who interact directly with the individual(s) in question. To have the freedom of thought and expression held in complete confidence is a gift to the spirit.

Collaboration is a key attribute of a curative culture. It creates common ground for success and accountability. For me, this idea summons a memory of the amazing collaboration and syncopation in the flight of the Artic Snow Geese that winter in the Skagit Valley, which sits about three hours north of Seattle, nestled between the Salish Sea and the Cascade Mountains in western Washington.

The Snow Geese are white-bodied with black tips on their wings and bills. Some 50,000 birds find their way into the Skagit Valley annually, resting and feeding away from their summer home on Wrangel Island in the Chukchi Sea just off the northeast coast of Russia. Once they arrive, the flocks' constant take-offs and landings create undulating white sheets that resemble linen flapping in the wind. Thousands of Snow Geese feed on the Fir Island delta formed by the North and South forks of the muddy Skagit River. But it's their flight that brings them to mind. The long trailing V's in the sky signal their arrival from the 6,900-mile journey from Wrangel Island. While in flight, they collaborate in a fascinating and distinctive manner that is unique to birds of this size. National Geographic describes the aerodynamics:

> "As a bird flaps, a rotating vortex of air rolls off each of its wingtips. These vortices mean that the air immediately behind the bird gets constantly pushed downwards (downwash), and the air behind it and off to the side gets

pushed upwards (upwash). If another bird flies in either of these upwash zones it gets a free lift. It can save energy by mooching off the air flow created by its flock-mate."[21]

It's no wonder that a highly collaborative coworker can be experienced as a breath of fresh air!

As desirable as collaboration can be, it would be quite understandable if a leader read the process described above and decided they do not have the time or patience for this remediation process. Admittedly, there is little to enjoy in the moment, and the outcome of this exercise is not entirely predictable. But for most, experience indicates that the sense of satisfaction comes from knowing they've been faithful to the culture they intend, embrace, and share. It also comes in seeing the "tone of the body" of the company maintain its equilibrium.

A curative culture seeks to allow for an environment where the curing or healing of the wounds we all carry from

---

[21] Ed Yong, "Birds That Fly in a V Formation Use an Amazing Trick," Science, January 15, 2014, https://www.nationalgeographic.com/science/article/birds-that-fly-in-a-v-formation-use-an-amazing-trick.

our toxic work experiences can occur. It is not the responsibility of the company's leadership, however, to enforce therapeutic practices upon their coworkers. We can only speak to coworkers' behaviors, not their feelings. The process described above is intended to identify some helpful insights and tools for leadership in remedying friction or disruptive behavior within the organization. Disruptive individual(s) are responsible for their behavior, realizations, and consequences. A curative culture allows them the *opportunity* to self-correct.

Thus far, in discussing curative culture, the lens has been focused upon those who bring disruption with them into the work community. Thankfully, most coworkers bring very little disruption with them. On the contrary, they generally bring their best selves to work most days. When coworkers feel safe, respected, and trusted in an environment of fairness, they will be more likely to respect and trust their coworkers and leaders.

Knowing what is expected in a work community and being adequately resourced to achieve it can create a feeling of well-being among coworkers. This alignment of expectations and resource allocation might be said to be a sacred balance. A curative work environment respects and fulfills the implied promises that clearly articulated expectations carry with them.

Adequately resourcing coworkers is a prime responsibility of leadership. It requires the ability to subjugate our urges to extract maximum profits from a work community. Admittedly, this patient practice often contradicts many of us living in capitalist cultures. However, it need not be a threat to profitability. It requires leadership to think in "long haul" terms that iconic investor Warren Buffet might appreciate. He is known for exercising patience in his investments.

The word "patience," when used as an adjective, can mean "steadfast despite opposition, difficulty, or adversity."[22] When used as a noun, "patient" can mean "an individual awaiting or under medical care and treatment."[23] In the context of describing a curative culture, both are useful.

The sacred balance implied in the appropriate alignment of coworker expectations, resource allocation, and profitability calls to mind the concept of "stewardship," which Merriam-Webster defines as "the careful and responsible management of something entrusted to one's care."

The Native peoples of the coastal Pacific Northwest, from what is today southern Alaska southward almost to the Columbia River, which separates Washington and Oregon, are sometimes referred to as "people of the cedar."[24] Versatile beyond European imagination, the people who have inhabited this world for centuries made use of every part of

---

[22] "Patient," in *Merriam-Webster Dictionary*, March 14, 2025, https://www.merriam-webster.com/dictionary/patient.

[23] Merriam-Webster, "Patient".

[24] Hilary Stewart, *Cedar: Tree of Life to the Northwest Coast Indians* (D & M Publishers, 2009).

the red and yellow cedar tree. It's been said that they were born under it, they wore it, they navigated the seas in canoes carved from it, they lived in houses made of it, they cooked their food in bentwood boxes, and when they died, cedar mortuary poles were made to commemorate them.[25] Their reverence for the stewardship of the environment that they depended upon to sustain them brings them to my mind. In a curative culture, leadership involves a high level of stewardship of the human resources entrusted to them.

Many years ago, I had the privilege of hiking on Meares Island, off the western coast of Vancouver Island, near the village of Tofino in British Columbia. It was here that I saw some of the largest old-growth cedars in the world. One bore the marks of living harvest, a blaze, if you will. Centuries before, Native women had cut into a young cedar and pulled a strip of bark from the living tree, leaving a large scar measuring roughly 14 inches wide by 20 feet tall. The

---

[25] Stewart, *Cedar: Tree of Life to the Northwest Coast Indians.*

bark and its soft inner lining had been taken to become containers for food, water, rope, string, clothing, or just about anything imaginable. To my amazement, I learned that "pulling bark" didn't harm or kill the tree! It had survived almost 1,000 years and would likely stand for many more centuries. The cedar tree sustained their lives. They knew that stripping a tree of most or all its' bark would have killed the tree and led to deforestation.

The Natives' reverence for cedar trees was matched by their reverence for everything within their environment. They had been taught from birth and experienced first-hand, the values of stewardship. At the time, there was no iron, bronze, or steel to provide tools, cooking pots, or utensils. They depended solely upon what the Creator, or in their belief system, the "Great Spirit," had given them in the awe-inspiring nature around them.

We can find much to embrace in the examples of

stewardship exhibited by Native cultures. Their under-standing of the precious balance of nature reminds us of the benefits of carefully stewarding what has been entrust-ed to us, including the lives we impact within our work community. Adequately resourcing the people we depend upon for profitability requires knowing when to invest in our company and when to take our hard-earned profit. A curative culture provides the fertile soil where meaningful work can become a thing of great beauty, resulting in both employee satisfaction and high levels of profitability.

7
THE COMMUNITY WE SHARE

If by our very presence, we change our environment, and it follows that each person added to a work community makes their own impression, it bears repeating that the community is impacted in some unique way, just by their presence. It's intriguing that organizations are the sum of the varying personalities working inside them.

When someone is investigating the possibility of becoming a coworker in an organization, they would do well to closely examine the company's values. This may be, after all, the key criteria for selecting a work community. It would be wise to move on if the values are not clearly articulated or perhaps non-existent. On the other hand, if the values are articulated, are they mutually beneficial, i.e., are they good for the company *and* the coworkers? In a curative culture, values are not hung on the wall or posted on a webpage and forgotten. They are put into practice beginning with the recruitment process. If the values largely state what the coworker owes the company, this is a key indicator of the company's existing culture.

Should the investigating person encounter values that are well articulated and mutually beneficial but not in alignment with their own beliefs and values, they will have a decision to make. Assuming they are invited to join this work community, is the "values gap" too great? False starts are difficult for all parties concerned. Choosing to "try out" a company in the hope of melding their values is high risk. Admittedly, it takes a person of significant character, discipline, and self-confidence to walk away from a position paying competitive wages. Perhaps the deciding factors in a situation like this are how well the vision and mission of the company compel further exploration.

On the other hand, when a company is investigating the possibility of hiring a person to become a coworker, they would do well to determine how well the individual's values align with those held by the company. Introducing a person with conflicting or unarticulated values into the sum of the varying personalities that exist most often results in a false start requiring significant recovery or repair.

In my mid-thirties, I found myself unemployed, partially by my own hand. My employer and I held very different views on how coworkers should be treated. His culture of intimidation and humiliation paralyzed me and many others in his agency. I tried to tough it out, but after one of the more devastating years of my life, I began to voice my opinions, and it didn't sit well.

He initiated our conversation about our differing viewpoints, which led to his asking, "Well, do we try to resolve our differences? Or do we part company?" I responded very quickly, "We part company!" He then commanded me to go clean out my desk. A sense of great relief flooded over me as I—almost gleefully—obliged.

It's important here to express the range of emotions that came with this liberating experience. As thrilled as I was to be out from under the weight of an abusive and authoritarian leader, there was still a sense of shame associated with packing up my office under the watchful eyes of my supervisor. It didn't help that I was escorted out of the building in full view of my coworkers with my file box of personal effects. The financial realities of unemployment also served as a temper to my relief.

The job market in Seattle was tough for a person with my skill set. Being a direct response fundraising consultant for nonprofit organizations would require that I find another agency that was hiring. Seattle didn't have many companies of this kind at the time, so I found myself interviewing with a start-up. The founder was not a pleasant sort, plus he offered me about 60% of what I had been earning. It wasn't a situation I wanted or could accept. My deep love of the Pacific Northwest and my family ties there made it difficult to think of leaving it to find another position in my field. However, the options there were so limited that I decided to look outside the fundraising realm and take my direct response skills to the commercial marketplace.

I found myself sitting in offices, trying to understand the nature of the companies I had found in the newspaper's "want ads." This was 1987, and the internet was still in its infancy and without public access. There were no websites or job boards I could scour.

One day, I interviewed with a company that built and sold semi-trucks. It was one of the major brands. The interview was going quite well, and the HR person clearly thought that I had the direct response skills they needed. Then, he leaned back in his chair, threw his pencil on his desk, and said, "Look, you are clearly qualified for this job. And if you can convince me that you will be happy selling trucks for a living versus raising money to feed hungry children, I'll hire you." His insight and honesty were disarmingly evident and accurate. He saw someone who could indeed "fill a slot," if you will, but he had more integrity than to hire a person whose values didn't match those of his own company. For me, it was a defining moment. He was right; I couldn't sacrifice my values and sense of calling for a paycheck. I would never have been happy generating sales leads for trucks through the mail. It would have been a short-term fix and a false start for both of us.

Admittedly, for me, it was also a time of significant confusion. With my consent, I had been walked out of an agency that existed to raise money for not-for-profits, the very thing I now know to be my calling in life. Yet the toxic authoritarian culture of that firm had suffocated my spirit. There were no viable options for me to live where I loved to be, close to so much natural beauty and close to family and friends. I felt the jagged edges of failure sticking out through my soul. If only I had been a different person, one that fit well with this firm located in my beloved corner of the world, things could have been very different. But I didn't fit.

What's more, I didn't want to fit into a place where employees quaked every time the owner returned to the office after being away for a few days. A place where standing in the owner's office meant only one thing: a barrage of insults and humiliation. I could not share who I was and what I could do in an environment of fear. By being in that firm, I was further upsetting its dysfunctional equilibrium. The owner knew it, and I knew it. Through the grapevine, I later learned that my colleagues there knew it, too. Not long after my unceremonious departure, a mass exodus occurred when an enterprising employee started her own agency, and most of the staff followed her. The company where I had experienced so much toxicity, over time, ceased to exist.

Again, if by our very presence, we change our environment, and it follows that each person added to a work community makes their own impression, the community is impacted in some unique way, just by their presence. It's intriguing that organizations are the sum of the varying personalities working inside them. My departure had not caused the mass exodus from that company. For those who remained behind, when another, more attractive opportunity had opened up, through the creation of the new agency, the work community moved to a much safer place.

After unsuccessfully trying to find meaningful work in my home state, it was time for me to pick up the phone. So, while I still had a modicum of self-respect, I reconnected with people who knew what I could do and respected me for who I was.

As hard as it was to cross the southern border of the Evergreen State, I soon found myself driving a Ryder truck filled with my family's belongings over the bridge spanning the great Columbia River. It hurt to look in the rearview mirror as we crossed into Oregon and see the truss bearing the "Welcome to Washington" sign disappearing in the distance as I began to make my way to a direct response fundraising firm near Dallas, Texas. I had been hired by an agency that knew me and my experience and was willing to pay me what I was worth.

During the 2,300-mile drive to Dallas, I reflected on my career to date. If not for that HR person's wisdom and integrity, I believe I would have taken that job marketing semi-trucks through the mail. His insights into the necessity of a values match revealed something about myself that I had not, until that interview, fully known. Even though my skills were a match for the job he had available, my values were not going to be a good fit for his company or my personal long-term satisfaction. He was being vigilant in the preservation of the culture of his company. The last thing he needed was a short-term hire who would have jumped at the opportunity when a better fit came along. What I had learned about myself was invigorating. I had learned that, for me, my career *was* my way to "give back." My future began to come more into focus as I passed each mile marker on my way to Dallas. It increased my appetite to marry my values with a company culture that I had not yet experienced. My values were best suited to raising money for not-for-profit ministries and organizations. I just needed the right culture to be able to make my contribution. I've never looked back again.

8
THE COMMUNITY WHERE WE THRIVE

My mother, Shirley Shaw, taught me many things that shaped my soul. She did this as an inconspicuous extension of her presence. Her influence came in the feelings of the safety she created for her children, the natural waves of conversation, the myriad stories she would tell over the course of a day, and the gentle teachings and guidance of a loving parent. It's the culture she created at home that serves as my model for a community that allows for acceptance, encouragement, and belief—a curative culture.

My father, Hobart Shaw, or "Buster" to his family and friends, was the very definition of the "hunter-gatherer." I've spoken about his brick laying trade, the marks it left on his body, and the lasting impression he left on the buildings in much of South Seattle. He also, out of necessity, was an accomplished deer and elk hunter. His .30/06 bolt-action rifle was always at the ready behind the bench seat of his Chevy pickup. With the use of his trowel, his rifle, and his skinning knife, he toiled to feed his family of six. His intelligence and creativity, coupled with his strongly tested survival instincts and my mother's contributions, formed so much of the person I bring to my work community.

This cursory telling of my own beginnings or family-of-origin story, is woven together with those of my coworkers to ultimately influence the culture of our work community. Simply put, each of us brings who we are into our work environment, and much of us is formed in our early, malleable years. The intrigue of it all is how many stories we each possess, and to a very high degree, how they possess us. It's fascinating to consider the resulting chorus of culture.

John Donne, in 1624, in his Meditation 17[26] writes:

No man is an island,
Entire of itself,
Every man is a piece of the continent,
A part of the main.
If a clod be washed away by the sea,
Europe is the less.
As well as if a promontory were.
As well as if a manor of thy friend's
Or of thine own were:
Any man's death diminishes me,
Because I am involved in mankind,
And therefore never send to know for whom the bell tolls;
It tolls for thee.

The curative culture where we thrive is a place where there is more than a small recognition that "every man is a piece of the continent." The accompanying sense of belonging gratifies and fortifies, enabling each sojourner to contribute from their own unique perspective. This is said without any illusion of finding or creating a utopian workplace, for as we all know, it doesn't exist. Rather, it is an expression

---

[26] John Donne, *Devotions Upon Emergent Occasions*, 1923.

of being in a community where a strong majority believes it is connected, and in that connectedness and interdependence is a part of what is right with the world. Donne says it so well, "Because I am involved with mankind."

I write these things with the knowledge that much of what I'm proposing is totally contrary to what many of us know as "the American way of life." Our watchword is independence rather than community. Our mantra is "self-made man" rather than being "involved in mankind." If we desire to step away from a toxic culture, we would do well to challenge the norm. I assure you that the destination will be well worth the journey.

Most of us have likely heard the expression, "If you love what you do, you'll never work a day in your life." Confucius, Marc Antony, and Mark Twain have all been credited with the origination of this oft-quoted insight. Today, it still leaves us thinking about those fortunate to have found what they love to do in the way of work. In the curative culture where we are given the opportunity to be our best selves, we can thrive. We might also consider the value of this additional thought: *if you love who you are at work, you will love being at work.*

Leaders who see the value in their employees and help them thrive have more fulfilling lives themselves. There are so many pressures to perform carried by those responsible for the bottom line, profitability being chief among them. With this pressure, the careful maintenance of a company's culture can be overlooked, pushed aside, or even sacrificed in the belief that maximum profits come at the expense of the individuals who help create them. When this occurs, employee "buy-in" to excellence diminishes, and with it, the quality of the company's product or services suffers. As we know, consumers can spot this loss in value quickly and shift their loyalties to your competitors. This only adds to the pressures of leadership. When leadership cares about their employees' well-being as well as the company's bottom line, their employees care more for each other and the well-being of where they work, and a thriving business is the result.

Unlike utopian aspirations, these feelings of connectedness to each other and the belief that the world is made better through each day's work can indeed exist. There is no expectation of perfection, or nirvana-like overtones at play here. There is, however, a commitment, by the work community, to a set of shared values and the determination to remain vigilant about, what Max De Pree refers to as, "the tone of the body."[27]

Vigilance, in this context, is meant to signify acute awareness of the work community's cultural health. Are there any toxic patterns of uncivil communications developing? Are disruptive behaviors beginning to impact group dynamics? Are there signs of chronic frustration or dissatisfaction? Is

---

[27] De Pree, *Leadership Is an Art.*

work performance flagging?

If indeed each of us participates in creating our work culture by bringing who we are to the community, then awareness of who each person is can be very useful in deciphering the signals contributing to the erosion of a curative culture within the work community.

This level of awareness is a community-wide endeavor, and it requires a basic sense of safety and fairness to communicate concerns. This leads us back to the fundamental well-being questions co-workers have about their colleagues and supervisors:

"Can I trust them and their intentions?" "Are they worthy of my respect?" "Am I safe?"

If coworkers respect their leaders and colleagues, trust their intentions, and feel safe in their work environment, then they will want to preserve this curative culture. And if their work community prizes the knowledge and worth of the individuals within it, coworkers will seek a restorative resolution to any behavior that threatens their sense of well-being.

Having acknowledged the imperfect nature of any work culture, we must also extend vigilance to those raising concerns about others' behaviors. Wisdom, prudence, and discernment become the guardrails for negotiating this terrain.

When concerns arise over coworker behavior, remediation must not be allowed to linger once verified. Experience teaches that allowing dysfunctional behavior to continue without redress erodes belief in the embodiment of values. Perhaps even more sobering is the likelihood that if the offending behavior is allowed to continue without challenge, it can be construed or misconstrued to be with managerial approval.[28] In other words, if leaders allow dysfunctional or abusive behavior to continue unchallenged, it will likely be

---

[28] Bill Frisby of Strengthening Leaders, personal conversation with author, date unknown.

read by employees as favoritism. If the offending employee is a high producer, it signals that profits outweigh fairness, which is toxicity at its finest. This failure to act threatens the company's morale, and ultimately, profitability will suffer as well.

It's worth noting that the fear of releasing a highly productive employee who is exhibiting dysfunctional behavior, is not enough reason to allow the dysfunction to continue.[29] Usually, the fear of losing a high performer is exaggerated beyond the reality of the situation. Experience has shown me that once the dysfunction is removed, those who remain will flourish. The leader often realizes, "I should have done this sooner."

The curative culture where a work community truly thrives minimizes distractions while freeing coworkers to invest heavily in achieving the vision, mission, and values that drive the company. The resulting profitability provides

---

[29] Bill Frisby of Strengthening Leaders, personal conversation with author, date unknown.

jobs and growth opportunities, which is what initially drew

employees to their work community.

9
A COMMUNITY OF WORK

"Opportunity is often missed because it
comes dressed in overalls and looks like work."
— **Thomas Edison**

For some, "having a good work ethic" may mean exceeding expectations in the amount of time a coworker commits to their workday. To others, it can be more about how quickly a task can be successfully completed. Many hold that a good work ethic is evidenced by a position of "whatever it takes" to be successful. Again, let's define our terms, "Work Ethic, Noun: a belief in work as a moral good: a set of values centered on the importance of doing work and reflected especially in a desire or determination to work hard."[30]

The question, "How do we develop our work ethic?"

---

[30]"Work Ethic," in *Merriam-Webster Dictionary*, March 16, 2025, https://www.merriam-webster.com/dictionary/work%20ethic.

is not new to this generation, but it requires understanding by every age. Left unanswered, it can be a source of grating polarity, frustration, and disillusionment. Attempting to answer this question has its own hazards, as the number of answers may equal the number of people in the discussion.

As a company owner, I expect my employees to work hard and strive for excellence. This is what they are being resourced to do. The more responsibility an employee carries, the more expertise, time, and energy they can devote to the company's success. I am under no illusions, however, that even those carrying significant responsibilities are also subject to their own interpretation of what working hard means. For example, leaders with small children at home have demands being made on them that those with grown children may not. Those providing spousal or parental care, experiencing chronic personal health issues themselves, or any other configurations of the human condition may not have an equal number of hours they can commit to work. But all of them can and are being called upon to commit to accessibility and responsiveness to myself and their peers. It's all a part of what leaders do, and it is essential to the success of any work culture. In a curative culture, however, a person's life circumstances are acknowledged, considered, and accommodated, as long as it results in excellence.

For some, the phrase "work ethic" implies a "live to work" lifestyle. This perspective often includes a rebutting phrase, "work to live," which may also be accompanied by the implication of the moral superiority of the latter position. The implication being that we, as workers, have a choice.

Suppose this is true, that we can choose to think and act in a way that suggests that we are able to create our own definition of work ethic, i.e., write our own ticket. In this scenario, the worker thinks and acts in concert with their beliefs. As long as the work community agrees with them, all appears compatible.

As we know, there are many instances where differing views of the meaning of work and their accompanying actions become a source of conflict. It doesn't take long for a company with a work ethic to ascertain the value a new colleague places on work. Conversely, a new coworker takes their own reading, and within a few weeks, they know the work culture of their new place of employment. If the match is poor, everyone loses. Since it's highly unlikely that a work community will change its work expectations for one new coworker, it falls to the new person to quickly adapt or seek employment elsewhere. False starts are both time-consuming and costly for all concerned.

Things become more difficult when a new person's work habits are less obvious, i.e., some or much of what they achieve meets expectations. Couple this with a positive attitude, and the employer's ability to ascertain a new employee's compatibility with the existing work culture becomes less certain. Assuming there is a functioning feedback loop, it can require several months to observe a new person's work performance, provide feedback, and monitor the situation to determine if they are making enough progress. In the interim, the new coworker and the work community invest time and convey knowledge to each other. Expectations must be met for an ongoing work relationship to endure over time.

There are other influences that can impact a work community's expectations. Economic conditions can play a significant role in work cultures. The Great Recession, occurring in the early 2000s, resulted in the loss of nearly 9 million jobs in the U.S.[31] and 400,000 in Canada.[32] Between December 2008 and December 2010, it's estimated that 1.8 million U.S. small businesses went under.[33] Perhaps the point is

[31]"U.S. Bureau of Labor Statistics," Bureau of Labor Statistics, February 22, 2017, https://www.bls.gov/.
[32]"Labour Force Information: Analysis—December 2009," n.d., https://www150.statcan.gc.ca/n1/pub/71-001-x/2009012/part-partie1-eng.htm.
[33]"Barbara Weltman, "10 Years After the Financial Crisis: The Impact on Small Business," Investopedia, February 27, 2023, https://www.investopedia.com/small-business/10-years-after-financial-crisis-impact-small-business/.

already made, but those who had jobs treasured them during this trying time. There was very little discussion about "living to work" versus "working to live."

The COVID-19 epidemic also greatly impacted work communities and cultures. According to the U.S. Bureau of Labor and Statistics:

"Total civilian employment, as measured by the Current Population Survey (CPS), fell by 21 million from the fourth quarter of 2019 to the second quarter of 2020, while the unemployment rate more than tripled, from 3.6 percent to 13.0 percent."[34]

Statistics Canada reported, an unemployment rateof 13.0% for April of 2020 and 13.7% for the following month.[35]

With the availability of the first vaccines on December 14, 2020, in both the U.S. and Canada, people began to be

[34]"Sean M. Smith and Roxanna Edwards, "Unemployment Rises in 2020, as the Country Battles the COVID-19 Pandemic," *Monthly Labor Review*, June 8, 2021, https://doi.org/10.21916/mlr.2021.12.

[35]"Government of Canada, Statistics Canada, "The Daily — Labour Force Survey, April 2020," April 8, 2020, https://www150.statcan.gc.ca/n1/daily-quotidien/200508/dq200508a-eng.htm.

called back to work in the months that followed. However, many North Americans did not return to a physical office for work. According to the U.S. Census Bureau, "Between 2019 and 2021, the number of people primarily working from home tripled from 5.7% (roughly 9 million people) to 17.9% (27.6 million people), according to new 2021 American Community Survey (ACS) 1-year estimates…" Statistics Canada reported similar trends for this same period. Still, it is worth noting there are differences in each country's definition of "work from home," (WFH) and Canada exerted more stringent WFH policies than did the United States.

Whether working in an office environment or from home, in a manufacturing plant or a retail establishment, whether economic conditions are bullish or bearish, there remain expectations within a work community as to the quality and quantity of work that is considered acceptable.

Clear communication of these expectations is essential to a curative culture.

Coworkers are likely the first to notice any variation from acceptable standards, because they are the ones who step in and cover for each other in times of illness, vacations, weddings, maternity leave, or bereavement. In any work culture, this is a normal part of living. Leadership is often the last to know when a coworker's performance is flagging.

Informal communications within workgroups have a self-monitoring component. In a toxic culture, this can work against unity, a feeling of safety, and productivity. Within a curative culture, this communication is more likely to reflect the vigilance coworkers exhibit toward each other. This self-care bond between coworkers, when exercised thoughtfully and in a non-destructive manner, can be a significant indicator of the cultural health of a work community.

When a coworker frequently or consistently falls short of acceptable standards, leadership will likely be made aware. At this critical juncture, how the situation is dealt with is, in essence, a request for intervention, but it is more than this; it is also a test. Will leadership facilitate restoring the quality and quantity balance needed to function at optimum levels? Are the espoused values of the work community going to be brought to bear upon this flagging performance?

This restatement of coworker questions about their leaders, "Can I trust them and their intentions?" "Are they worthy of my respect?" "Am I safe?" might be appropriate here. Other questions of leadership that may not be fully known or articulated yet contribute to coworkers' sense of well-being, such as, "Are they fair?" "Are they interested in the facts of the situation as well as the feelings?" "Are the perspectives of the workgroup, including the person who has flagging performance, being considered?" Perhaps equally important is the question, "Are they really going to deal with this this time?" As referenced earlier, the failure of leadership to promptly address dysfunction within the work community may lead coworkers to assume leadership is not serious in their articulation of values, or at the very least, there is favoritism at play.

Vital work communities need coworkers who solve problems, not create them. If a coworker is not solving problems, they are contributing to their creation. Occupying a seat in a workgroup and performing below acceptable standards is demoralizing at best and undermines confidence in the values being espoused.

I did not sleep much during the night. In the morning, I would rise, shower, shave, get dressed, and try to eat breakfast. Almost by rote, my day would begin as I would drive across town to my office, and then I was going to absolutely ruin someone's life! These feelings and thoughts ran through me as I lay there with my head on the softness of my pillow.

At 29, I had found leading a team of six people intimidating. Ron was a very engaging and eager candidate. He showed up to his interview well-dressed, sported a smile, and had an energetic bounce to his step. Coupled with these attributes, he had interviewed extremely well. Unfortunately, I had very little experience in my new role and had little basis for formulating the requirements of the position I was trying to fill.

Within two weeks of Ron's hire, I was beginning to feel a growing knot in my stomach. After every meeting with him, I would sit in my office and reflect upon our conversations. Each experience left me with an increasing sense of dread that I had been too hasty in hiring Ron. His lack of knowledge of the market we were serving was becoming alarmingly apparent. My colleagues knew it, too. I could hear their doubts in the silence following my mention of his name. The involuntary aversion of their eyes when encountering him in the hallway only contributed to my angst.

When Jim, the Vice President of our workgroup, took me out to lunch, I felt something was up. After settling into our chairs, we ordered iced tea and began scanning the menu that we already knew by heart. Slowly and with feigned innocence, he posed the question the entire company was asking: "So how's Ron doing?" Quickly setting down my menu, I looked at Jim's grizzled face and blurted out, "Not well! I'm afraid..." Then I looked down at the table in shame. "I think I blew it, Jim," I said with evident remorse. "Happens to all of us," Jim replied, "It's all a part of new leader syndrome." He paused and said, "I've lost count of how many bad hires I've made." My head snapped up, "Really? It's like, uh, a thing?" "Yes," Jim said, "It's a rite of passage.

Welcome to Leadership 101." And then he smiled as he said, "The key is, what are you going to do about it?"

When I arrived at work the next morning, I tried to move swiftly into my office without making eye contact with anyone, especially Ron. I felt like the hangman, passing his quarry in the crowd who had gathered for the main event. After stowing my winter coat, scarf, and hat on the coat tree, I slid into my chair and studied the yellow notepad on my desk. My heart was pounding in my ears. The lack of sleep was already giving me that tingly feeling of exhaustion that visited the back of my neck. I needed coffee, but I wasn't about to leave my office to get it. So, I picked up my phone and called my assistant. "Uh, good morning, Jeanne. Do you think you could bring me a cup of coffee this morning? And tell Ron I'd like to meet with him at 4 o'clock today, ok?"

Taking my new gold Cross pen, a gift from Jim on my recent appointment, I began to sip my coffee. As the caffeine kicked in, my eyes began to clear enough to write down what I was going to say to Ron later that afternoon...

By 3:45, I was sure that I wasn't cut out for leadership! I had spent the day thinking of how my words would reverberate through this smiling, energetic man and wreak havoc on his life. In 15 minutes, Ron was going to hear the words that no one wants to hear, "I'm going to have to let you go." In 16 minutes, he'd be thinking, "What am I going to say to my wife?"

Ron appeared at my door promptly at 4. I asked him to close the door, and I saw from the look in his eyes that he knew what was coming...

I cried on my way home that evening, wiping my eyes on my coat sleeves. My attempts to compose myself at stoplights were not all that successful, which made pulling into my garage even more attractive. Walking through the back door and into the kitchen, I began a full-on sob. Leaning against the kitchen table, with one hand, I reached for a napkin with the other.

Around 7:00 p.m., I was standing in the kitchen drying the dinner dishes. I jumped as the phone rang. Nodding to my wife to answer it, I listened in horror as she extended the phone to me and said quietly, "It's Ron."

It was a conversation that lasted maybe 90 seconds, but it has stayed with me for the rest of my life. Ron called to thank me for all he had learned in the past few weeks and that he understood why I had let him go. He thanked me for helping him to see that this job was not the place for him. He had known it, too.

The heaviness in my head, shoulders, and chest all released and floated upward through the kitchen ceiling and beyond. I put my head back, exhaled a long and cleansing breath, and began crying the tears of the forgiven. It wasn't divine forgiveness, it wasn't Ron's forgiveness, it was mine.

I was forgiving myself for hiring someone who I should not have said "yes" to. All I could do now was hope to learn from my lack of experience and be more careful going forward.

When coworkers struggle to produce the required quantity or quality of work, they know it. How they decide to remedy the situation can determine their standing within the work community. In a curative culture, help can be given if they ask. Suppose they decide to continue in their current behavior, hoping no one will notice or challenge them to more acceptable performance levels. In that case, they have left the burden of corrective action to their colleagues. It's unknown if Ron was ever going to ask for help. What is known is that he knew he was not a good fit for his position. He also had the quality of character to pick up the phone and acknowledge that the decision to solve the problem, while difficult, was mutually beneficial.

Defining the culture of work is the sacred province

of those who lead work communities. To reiterate, all work community members bring their own contributions. However, it is the implied *duty* of leaders to clearly enunciate and embody the preferred culture of the work community. Perhaps it's not too bold to suggest that leaders of work communities, when seeking to build or maintain a curative culture, maintain a posture of *feverish vigilance* to ensure the community's work ethic.

For many coworkers, work ethics are ingrained in them. They are part of their family of origin story. Such was the case with Philip Stanhope, the 4th Earl of Stanhope. Writing advice to his son, "Whatever is worth doing at all is worth doing well."[36] Many of us in the workforce today grew up with Stanhope's words ringing in our ears. We likely heard the revised version, "Anything worth doing is worth doing well," and we attributed it to our parents, who were most likely the vocal party in this exchange.

---

[36]The Editors of Encyclopaedia Britannica, "Philip Stanhope, 4th Earl of Chesterfield | Biography & Facts," Encyclopedia Britannica, July 20, 1998, https://www.britannica.com/biography/Philip-Stanhope-4th-Earl-of-Chesterfield.

Some, particularly those who have grown up in poverty and have achieved some level of success, attribute their work ethic to an expression of gratitude for the accomplishments they have achieved in the face of great disadvantages, and for the kindnesses extended to them along the way.

Many of our parents, grandparents, or great (great) grandparents endured the deprivations of The Great Depression. They often referred to this worldwide economic catastrophe that took place from 1929 to 1941[37] as "The Hungry 30's." Considered the greatest economic downturn in modern history, it began with the U.S. stock market crash in 1929 and spread to the entire world. It was a shared deprivation that left its mark on the "builder generation" psyche, leaving many to spend their entire work life at the same employer. Financial security and food security were so closely linked that having a job was given more priority than upward mobility.

To many Depression-era survivors, work ethic meant,

---

[37]"Time Period: The Great Depression | Federal Reserve History," n.d., https://www.federalreservehistory.org/time-period/great-depression.

in the vernacular, "keeping your head down and your nose clean." In other words, it meant working hard and not causing trouble. Other common phrases reflecting the times were, "We're lucky to have a roof over our heads" and "At least we have food on the table." Perhaps the gallows humor of the time was never more evident than in the phrase, "You could buy anything you wanted for a nickel…but nobody had a nickel." My father's favorite was, "We were so poor we couldn't pay attention." It was no wonder that this "greatest generation" responded to those who chose to "drop out" in the 1960's with the refrain, "Get a job!" For those experiencing unprecedented deprivation during the final decades of the industrial age, work was the very essence of life; work was good. Having a "decent-paying job" was something to be treasured. It gave meaning to "getting up in the morning," and truthfully, it remains so today.

However, in a curative culture, the word "work"

requires redefinition. Work is not only a place to make a living but also a cherished place to make meaning in your day. It's how you spend the currency of your life.

10
A COMMUNITY OF OPPORTUNITY

"Hope is the thing with feathers that perches
in the soul – and sings the tunes without
the words – and never stops at all"[38]
— **Emily Dickinson**

In the steep evergreen-covered hills above Maple
Valley Highway, situated between Mt. Rainier to the south
and Seattle to the north, there is a place that has left an
indelible mark upon my soul. If you were to visit there
today, you would find horses grazing in a lush field of grass
surrounded by alder, fir, and cedar trees. This quiet place
once held the very center of my life in its hands.

We were a family of six. My mom, dad, and three
sisters were my constant companions in the 25-by-25
foot cabin erected there. Close quarters would be a severe
understatement, but we "made do." At the time, we had

---

[38]"Emily Dickinson, Hope Is the Thing With Feathers: The Complete Poems of Emily Dickinson (Women's Voice, 2019).

no other option.

In most ways, the word "cabin" implied a dignity that only an optimist would have used. Stenciled on the outside of the plywood exterior were the words: BOEING AIRCRAFT COMPANY. My dad had bought the structure from his nephew Barnie, who lived around the corner and down the road. I remember going with my dad to pick it up. The cabin was lying flat on a trailer, like a collapsed cardboard box, and was ready to reassemble. Barnie and his family had previously lived in it and finally upgraded to a contractor-built home. Now, he wanted to get it out of his yard.

We were happy to have it, and I worked with my dad to build a post-and-beam structure for it to rest on concrete blocks at the four corners. My contribution largely consisted of handing my dad tools, nails, and his old yellow sweatshirt, with its frayed collar and cuffs. He needed it when the clouds closed ranks, covering the sun, and the

Northwest chill crept back in among the surrounding trees, sword ferns, salal, and blackberry bushes.

By this time, I was about to enter the third grade and could read. I spent many winter afternoons lying on the plywood floor of that cabin near the oil stove, listening to the sound of rain on the roof while reading stories about great men like Abraham Lincoln, Booker T. Washington, and George Washington Carver. All from very humble beginnings, these men had grown in knowledge and stature to become three of the finest leaders ever produced by our country.

Even at this early age, I felt a sense of kinship with them in their poverty. Reading about their rise created a mysterious anticipation of my own future. These feelings were only partially based upon visions of grandeur. After all, what was the likelihood a kid like me could grow up to be president, like Abraham Lincoln, anyway? Mostly,

I felt inspired by a growing sense of hope that something better might be possible.

This hope carried me through many years of my family's moving from place to place, often crisscrossing the country from the Pacific Northwest to the Midwest and back. By the time I had completed my education, I had attended 19 different schools.

After graduating High School in Central Washington's northern Okanagan Valley, in the small border town of Oroville, I began to flounder a bit. As summer was ending, I had failed to save enough money to begin college. Working three jobs in my senior year in high school was still not enough to keep gas in the car, clothes on my back, and pay for college tuition, too. I'm quite certain that there was a bit of fiscal mismanagement on my part as well.

Just as I was about to give in to the currents swirling about me to remain in this small town to pick apples and pump gas, I was unexpectedly given an infusion of hope by Mrs. Walters, the mother of a high school friend. Having spent the previous night listening to rock and roll with her son, Steve, I had accepted the invitation to spend the night. As I prepared my goodbyes in the morning, Mrs. Walters asked me, "Where are you going to college this fall, Doug?" I shifted visibly and answered, "Oh, I've been accepted at Central, but I don't have the money. I'll have to start in January." She saw me for what I was: a kid about to give up on a college education. This diminutive woman looked up at me and asked, "How much is your first quarter's tuition?" Rather sheepishly, I answered, "A hundred and forty-five dollars." She moved quickly to her roll-top desk, sat down, and wrote a check for the full amount. Standing up, she thrust the check toward me and said, "There, now you have no excuse. And I want you to pay it back!" Her caring and generosity propelled me forward as I entered Central

Washington State College in Ellensburg that fall.

As I reflect, hope carried me on its back when I needed it most, onward to the calling awaiting me. Nine years later, I not only graduated from college but had also completed graduate school at Fuller Seminary in Pasadena, California.

This accomplishment ultimately led me to an opportunity for a career in raising funds for faith-based nonprofit organizations in the U.S. and Canada. For 10 years, as our children were born and began their own journeys, I worked as a fundraiser for nonprofits and the agencies that served them. During this time, I realized that to actualize my hopes of providing a better standard of living for my family and creating the work culture that I dreamed of, I would need to experience ownership. I founded my own fundraising firm, Douglas Shaw & Associates, 30 years ago at the time of writing, and today it continues to serve high-impact nonprofits. Many of the organizations our company serves exist to help the homeless, poor, hungry, and addicted. Most of the people receiving help are desperate for spiritual as well as physical hope. Lying on that plywood floor, reading under a rain-spattered roof, had been the spark that ignited years of preparation, ultimately enabling me to see and grasp the opportunity that became my life's work.

Opportunity, a close companion of hope, is the proving ground of our awareness. What do I mean by this? If we have the hope that life will get better or more gratifying, it's then likely that we'll begin looking for opportunities to make this happen. Our awareness of the possibilities that present themselves to us makes us hunger and thirst for opportunities when they arise.

Young Abraham Lincoln was always looking for opportunities. That was one of the many things that drew me to him. As a child, we shared some things in common; for instance, after his family moved to Indiana from Kentucky, hoping to find a better life, they first lived in a "half-faced camp." This three-sided shelter, about fourteen feet square, had a dirt floor and was open to the elements on one side.[39] It made my family's Boeing Packing Crate cabin look plush. Lincoln's limited access to school, while much starker than my own situation, helped me appreciate the continually interrupted schooling I received. And his voracious appetite for reading was a shared interest as well. Lincoln's continual striving for a better life bonded me to his character more than anything else. He was constantly on the lookout for opportunities to improve his circumstances.

We all need hope and the sense of security and betterment that opportunity provides. Therefore, it's not unexpected that many coworkers need to be assured that growth opportunities exist. However, it is imperative that *they* realize their own role in recognizing, being adequately prepared,

---

[39]David Herbert Donald, *Lincoln* (Simon and Schuster, 1995).

and accepting opportunities when they arise.

In a curative culture, a community of opportunity allows for a constant state of redefinition, of words, ideas, design, and, when prudent, the realignment of talent. There is an understandable difference between predictable expectations and stagnation. So it is with coworkers, who need both the predictable expectations that allow for reliability and the upward mobility required to inspire, enabling them to reach their potential.

A community of opportunity knows where it's heading but is not wedded to how to get there. Although rare, seismic shifts can occur, resulting in the creation of opportunities that cannot be foreseen, it is incumbent upon coworkers to be willing to accept redefinition and realign accordingly.

> "We must be willing to
> let go of the life we have planned, so as to
> have the life that is waiting for us."
> **E.M. Forster**

Curative cultures know the difference between reliability and opportunity, but there is also an acute awareness of the difference between opportunity and opportunism. Opportunity is defined as forward movement with thoughtfulness and civility, while the opportunism occurs regardless of the cost to those being impacted.

Opportunity is the co-mingling of hope and expectation with proactive and prudent pursuit. For many of us, it feels like the reward for being in the right place at the right time. This might be true, but it may also be part of a grand design to accomplish the goodness and justice that people of goodwill long to see in this world.

11

A COMMUNITY OF EXCELLENCE

The leaders of a work community have another duty that all too often flies in the face of conventional wisdom. They must own the reality that achieving excellence, which is an elusive quality because it rises above the norm, does not always maximize profits in the short term. This is something many corporations today can find unacceptable, but not Berkshire Hathaway.

Excellence is something the late Charlie Munger helped billionaire Warren Buffet to value.

> "He weaned me away from the idea of buy-
> ing very so-so companies at very cheap prices,
> knowing that there was some small profit
> in it, and looking for some really wonderful
> businesses that we could buy in fair prices,"
> Buffet told CNBC in May 2016.

This same article continues,

"An early example of the shift was illustrated in 1972 by Munger's ability to persuade Buffet to sign off on Berkshire's purchase of See's Candies for $25 million even though the California candy maker had annual pre-tax earnings of only about $4 million. It has since produced more than $2 billion in sales for Berkshire."[40]

It may take years to build a culture of excellence. It may even take several years. In my company, we have a saying, "If it was easy, anyone could do it!" As Merriam-Webster[41] defines excellent, "very good of its kind: eminently good: FIRST CLASS," this investment of time becomes more palatable. If you were to read these words and abandon the concept of pursuing excellence, you would not be alone. Many, if not most, corporations have already chosen to sacrifice quality for immediate financial gain. But since you've read this far, perhaps you are looking

[40]"Martin Steinberg, "Charlie Munger, Investing Genius and Warren Buffett's Right-hand Man, Dies at Age 99," CNBC, November 29, 2023, https://www.cnbc.com/2023/11/28/charlie-munger-investing-sage-and-warren-buffetts-confidant-dies.html.

[41]"Excellent," in *Merriam-Webster Dictionary*, March 16, 2025, https://www.merriam-webster.com/dictionary/excellent.

for something different in your work life. It might be that you value the feel of true craftsmanship in your hands or the pleasant surprise of encountering exceptional service and possibly the close attention to detail in a well-built home. Excellence impresses us, and in a company, it inspires both the customer and the people who work there.

Like many who begin life in extreme poverty yet long for more, I had to find ways to finance my education on my own. My parents wanted me to attend college but knew they could not contribute. It was literally a struggle for them to keep the lights in our home turned on. There were many times growing up when I bore the embarrassment of having friends stop by near the end of the day and ask me why there were no lights on in my house. I would look down at the ground and stammer something about our family wanting to save money by not using too much electricity. I was too embarrassed to tell them that the power company had cut off our electricity for lack of payment. So, paying for my education was not something I ever expected from my parents. I knew my only viable path was to work my way through school.

During college, I held many jobs to pay for my tuition, books, and housing. I worked in an Army-Navy Surplus store after class but often found higher-paying jobs during the summer break. As horrifying as it sounds, one summer I became the slaughterer in a sheep packing plant, making $10 an hour (much better than the $3.65 per hour minimum wage jobs I had been working).

I still cherish the day when I received a letter from my dad. I'm not certain he had ever written a letter before, and certainly not one meant for me. I was worried as I opened it, fearing something may be wrong with my mom, who was the letter-writer in our family. Inside the small envelope was a two-page letter in my father's shaky script. He had written to encourage me in my studies, offering advice about listening to the still, small voice of God for direction in my life. He also included the only financial contribution he could or would ever make towards my education…a 20 dollar bill. It reminded me of the "widow's mite" in the Bible, where Jesus lifted up her offering of two copper coins because she gave them out of her poverty.[42] The still, small voice used this letter and gift to nudge me along to become the only member of my immediate family to complete a college education.

Upon graduating in 1975, I readied myself for another step in my education: graduate school. I had been accepted at Fuller Seminary in Pasadena, California, meaning I would need to make a significantly higher wage to pay for graduate-level tuition and books. Since I had done some house painting while in college, when a friend invited me to paint apartments with him in Pasadena, I leaped at the opportunity.

---

[42]Luke 21:1-4, The Holy Bible

We were paid for every apartment we completed rather than by the hour, so we hustled to finish one each day. It was not inspiring work. We often arrived at our assigned apartment only to discover mounds of garbage filling the place. Grumbling, we would kick the trash into the center of a room so we could paint the walls around it. It was demoralizing to paint apartments that had been so poorly treated by their inhabitants and badly maintained by their owners. After a few weeks, my painting partner decided to do something else to make money, and I decided it was time to work on something that truly inspired me.

I visited a contractor I knew who was familiar with my capabilities as a painter. He encouraged me to serve a different market, high-end homes in South Pasadena and San Marino. Through his connections, I began working on beautiful manor houses and sprawling mid-century properties. As the word spread and referrals increased, I started hiring my fellow students from Fuller and eventually had a crew of eight working full-time during the summer months. One day, while lying on my stomach on the floor of a butler's pantry, carefully using a small sable brush to apply navy blue pin-striping to the leaded glass trim on bright white cabinets, I realized that I had chosen not to just cover things with paint but rather to become excellent in my painting skills. By working on these beautiful homes, I gained an appreciation for quality workmanship that has followed me everywhere I have worked since.

I have also seen that when people are called to excellence, they rise to the occasion. It is important to note that leaders cannot simply mandate excellence. Rather, it must be modeled through thoughtful adherence to identified values, clarity of communication, and the willingness to remove all obstacles that do not align with those values. It takes an immensely committed work community to successfully rise after falling, failing, or being knocked down. However, excellence is much more than standing back up; it's the refinement of thought and action over time, tempered by the fires of failure, and learning to find the necessary footing to minimize the possibility of a stumble. When mistakes occur, the primary question is, "Is this a rare occurrence?" or "Is this a systemic issue?" As we know, excellence is not perfection but rather a high standard around which to rally. When the stumbles do occur, the loss is acknowledged, perhaps even mourned, but only for a very short time. In a community of excellence, mistakes become teaching moments that instruct the work community.

Individual excellence comes through belief in the values that guide the work community, trust in the fairness of leadership, and reciprocal respect and civility from peers. Therefore, it follows that those with an appetite for being the best are only satisfied when there is an established pattern of success so predictable that it has become a lifestyle of greatness.

Individual excellence or greatness is at its best when it becomes the servant of the work community. Those who experience what Greenleaf calls the "Journey into the nature of legitimate power and greatness"[43] have eyes to see the life-changing benefits of helping their employees and coworkers succeed.

Work communities exhibit excellence when there is the will, expectation, and proven track record of the melding of outstanding individual efforts into an organism of greatness. In a curative culture, the footprints of all the individuals in the work community evince a syncopation of movement that resembles an elegant dance.

Sadly, a word of warning is necessary here. While it may require years to create a culture of excellence, it can take just a few short months or years to turn an excellent

---

[43]Greenleaf, *Servant Leadership.*

work community into a solely profit-focused, culturally toxic enterprise. The pressures of leading a publicly traded business can reduce a vision for excellence to a near-sighted Q1, Q2, Q3, and Q4 maximum earnings-driven myopia. This is not just a phenomenon in publicly traded companies. It is equally tempting for privately held firms to engage in this judgment-blinding behavior.

When a work community allows itself to become solely focused on financial performance versus creating a magnificent product or service, the losses in human trust and resources and consumer confidence can become almost irreversible. Once this occurs, even those board members and stockholders with myopic attitudes for profit at all costs turn upon the leaders of the once excellent work community. Shedding their own culpability, they now seek answers to the question, "How could standards have been allowed to deteriorate to current levels?" For those leading the work community, this is not the time to challenge authority. It's simply too late.

Speaking truth to power is where exceptional leaders earn their keep and, perhaps equally important, their sense of self-respect and reputation. In a community of excellence, the trust created by values-driven leadership creates a sense of balance, fairness, and reality-based thinking that encourages coworkers to respectfully speak (truth) to all levels of leadership (power).

The wisdom required to anticipate or recognize the sometimes subtle shifts in thinking that can threaten a community of excellence comes from a place of a deep-seated sense of truth, integrity, and, sometimes, expendability. Leaders in a curative culture have an exceptional grasp of the nuanced balance required to maintain the cultural equilibrium of a work community. They are constantly on guard, watching for the degradation of values, the lapses in discipline, and the straying from reality that lead to mediocrity. These same leaders are acutely aware that the threats to excellence can come from within the work community or from the clients or customers it serves who choose to exert their will in contrast to the facts.

Choosing when to respectfully speak truth to power is a divine moment that, even if ignored, is a model of great character and life-changing inspiration for those with ears to hear. It is also, for the one speaking, a deeply rewarding contribution to living a life without regret. For those in power, it is a test of their character at minimum and a challenge to aspire to legitimate greatness at its best.

Several years ago, my company was making a sales pitch to a large nonprofit in New York. We had been invited to participate in this Request for Proposal (RFP) process to provide direct mail and online fundraising services, and we knew it would be a highly competitive situation. Our team assembled a few minutes early in the prospect's offices. We chose to spread out around the very long boardroom table, making sure there were spaces between our team members for their team members to fill in when they entered the room.

When the prospect's team arrived, they were very warm in their greeting. We chatted for a few minutes and then took our places. As we began, the door opened, and the CEO unexpectedly entered the room. Everyone stood. I made my way over to him and shook his hand. His team seemed surprised to see him, as were we, as he had made it clear to them that he would not be in attendance because the decision to hire an agency was theirs to make. As we returned to our seats, the CEO chose a seat near the head of the table to my left. He nodded, and the meeting resumed. About 10 minutes into the presentation, the CEO could no longer contain himself. He blurted out his disappointment in our presentation. Turning toward him, I could see the looks on the faces of his team. They seemed disappointed, too, but their disappointment was in the behavior of their CEO. He continued his condemnation by saying, "You haven't shown me ANYTHING I haven't seen before! I was hoping you'd have some new special nugget for us, BUT I GUESS NOT." "Would you like me to stop?" I asked. "No, continue on. Just know you have ten minutes left to impress me." I felt disrespected and angry but somehow managed to contain myself and remain surprisingly calm. Everyone watched to see my next move. Leaning forward over the table, I looked down past the people seated next to me and directly into the eyes of the CEO. "You know, Sam, if you are looking for a 'special nugget,' I don't think the next ten minutes will reveal one. What you will hear is our honest take on where we believe you are, according to your own data, and where we can help." He responded, "You have nine minutes..." Looking down at the surface of the table, I had made my decision. Closing my leather folder, I looked around the table at my team as if to say, "We're done here." Standing up, I told the CEO, "Sam, there is no special nugget or 'silver bullet' to improve your fundraising. Only a clear-eyed examination of the facts and the employment of the sound fundamentals of direct response will give you the performance improvement you seek. Thank you for taking the time to meet with us today." And with that, we said our goodbyes to his team and made our way to the elevator. There was sadness in the eyes of those employees who shook our hands. Some of them mouthed the words, "I'm so sorry."

It may come as no surprise that the CEO did not come to a good end. His roughshod treatment of his staff had led to significant turnover in the company. I later heard how his dismissal directly resulted from his unwelcome behavior toward the women on his team.

Excellence comes to those who are willing to pay the price. While there is undoubtedly a monetary implication, it is so much more than this. Excellence stems from the belief that there is meaning in living according to our values, even at the price of personal cost and sacrifice. While our meeting with the prospect in New York never resulted in winning business from them, I learned the meeting had made a significant impression on all the present staff, both on their team and mine. It also made a significant impression on me. I saw myself use a level of self-control that was beyond my norm. Because I had not lashed out, I had not *become the issue* in this situation. It required everything I had to say a polite "thank you" to the CEO at the termination of our presentation. When I left that boardroom, I had no regrets about how I had conducted myself. It gave me a newfound confidence to know that I could go toe-to-toe with an intensely strong-willed person and maintain my self-respect. That day, I had spoken truth to power in a manner that has served me well ever since.

As a CEO myself, I greatly respect and depend upon those who are willing to risk *respectfully* telling me things I don't necessarily want to hear. It's important to underscore the quality of respect when taking this type of risk. Words, tone, and timing, when steeped in the attitude of respect, can result in a career-defining moment that distinguishes an excellent employee from a capable one.

A culture of excellence can also positively impact coworkers in ways that their leaders may never know. The "pride of ownership" in doing something well is a reward, but it can be eclipsed by the sense of belonging to something of great significance. Being a part of something that is *right with the world* is a soul-nourishing experience that should not be underestimated.

The quality of excellence in a curative culture applies

not only to the treatment of people in our workplace but also to the crafting of the goods and services we create. Our co-workers know that when we set expectations of excellence, accept nothing else, and remove all obstacles to achieving it, excellence will become "the way we do things around here."

Many years ago, I worked for a fundraising agency in Dallas, Texas. It was known for having top expertise in strategic thinking and creative execution. One of the owners, Jim Killion, was also our Executive Creative Director. It was Jim who modeled excellence for the company. If a fundraising campaign could satisfy Jim, the results would shine, and everybody knew it. He would invest his time in you if he sensed that you wanted to achieve excellence. To this day, I remember, use, and model many of the skills he taught me. Jim's legacy of excellence lives on in the standards practiced in my own company.

As we know, excellence is seldom experienced in a strictly cost-driven environment. Consumer intolerance for rising prices leaves most businesses searching for ways to "do more with less." This sentiment has led most companies to compromise the quality of their products and services. The oft-heard phrase, "they don't make'em like they used to," is a testament to much of society's acceptance of the lower standards experienced today. A commitment to excellence enables us to see this as an opportunity to do what others are unwilling to do. After all, "if it was easy, anyone could do it!"

12
A COMMUNITY OF GENEROSITY

An open hand. It carries with it a sense of trust, comfort, and, yes, generosity. As with all things, an open hand can also be an acknowledgment of stewardship. For the caring leader, this can imply that what we hold has been placed there for our own use, guardianship, and the extended hand of sharing.

Perhaps the greatest act of generosity in a work community is to provide a sense of purpose to those we lead and serve alongside. All great endeavors seem to require participants to join in a deeply held singular purpose.

I have often admired the clarity displayed upon the sides of the long-haul trucks for Old Dominion Freight Line, "Helping the world keep promises."[44] The clarity of purpose encapsulated in these simple words inspires confidence that

---

[44] Old Dominion Freight Line, "LTL Freight Shipping & Logistics Services | ODFL," n.d., https://www.odfl.com/.

this company understands why it exists.

In a community of generosity, it is incumbent upon leadership to help coworkers understand that they are "part of what is right with the world."[45] To do this, leaders must understand their company's contribution to society. Granted, this may be less of an effort for some than others. Understanding societal contribution may require stepping back to see the end use of the product being created. For example, at Douglas Shaw & Associates, as a direct response fundraising firm, we apply our efforts to determine how best to communicate to people (donors) who have the desire to help others in need. Once the nonprofits we serve approve our ideas, we write words and design images for digital, on-air, and print communications that motivate donors to give. But this is not the end of what we do. The result does not come when our message is aired, posted, or mailed. The results of our actions are only fully realized when hungry

---

[45]Douglas Shaw & Associates, "Direct Response Fundraising for Nonprofits," October 24, 2024, https://www.douglasshaw.com/.

people are fed, people in poverty are lifted up in body and spirit, and when the good news of faith is shared through the organizations we serve. Understanding and communicating this to our staff gives meaning to their long work hours. Helping a work community to gain a complete understanding of the impact of their work is a generous act.

The generosity of spirit found in a curative culture is part of its essence. Amidst all the expectations of excellence, work ethic, and integrity there also lie feelings of compassion, caring, and a desire for all to succeed both personally and professionally. While this is no small task, it allows a company's leadership to live without regret for how they have treated those who look to them for direction. I like to think of this as the Fezziwig Principle.[46]

Another quality to consider, freedom of thought, might appear self-evident; it is not always so. In a curative culture, it is an exercise to be encouraged. The generosity

---

[46]Charles Dickens, *A Christmas Carol*, 1858.

of being encouraged to be oneself and to think for oneself provides a foundation for the diversity of personhood and ideas that feed creativity and innovation. This great freedom, when seasoned by the intentional practice of civility, contributes to the overall health of the work community. For some leaders, freedom of thought might feel threatening as it may, to them, mean "all ideas are good ideas" and, therefore, must be embraced and acted upon. Not at all. Ideas in themselves indicate that the work community is engaged and willing to problem solve and create. However, it is incumbent upon leadership to provide context and insight when an idea is accepted or rejected. Dismissing an idea without explanation invalidates the belief that freedom of thought is encouraged.

The adage, "knowledge is power,"[47] often attributed to Sir Francis Bacon, informs those seeking to be generous with information within in a work community. Perhaps

---

[47]"In His 'Meditationes Sacrae' Francis Bacon Writes 'Ipsa Scientia Potestas Est' (Knowledge Is Power): History of Information," n.d., https://www. historyofinformation.com/detail.php?id=5253.

making a slight revision to "knowledge empowers" would be more in keeping with a curative culture. In my view, expectations of greatness carry obligations of the generosity of knowledge. Appropriately communicated information not only enlightens and empowers coworkers; it helps to minimize unproductive and often inaccurate speculation.

Having encountered many who believe that "people should be kept on a need-to-know basis," it has become evident that Benjamin Franklin's *Poor Richard* was correct, "Three may keep a secret if two of them are dead."[48] The proverbial grapevine is omnipresent. Being human, the work community is constantly sharing information, and speculation abounds in the absence of intentionality and accuracy. Speculation can become a very close companion to toxicity if left undiluted by reality.

Another by-product of the need-to-know basis philosophy emerges when knowledge is used to control, at

---

[48]"Poor Richard's Almanack – Benjamin Franklin Historical Society," n.d. http://www. benjamin-franklin-history.org/poor-richards-almanac/.

worst, or perhaps a reward for the privileged few. At best, it can create a dark currency within the work community. It can lead those "in the know" to manipulate or abuse their coworkers.

This is not to say all coworkers should be privy to all aspects of corporate finance, human resource issues, or the like. Within a work community, there is a need to receive reality-based information that is commensurate with the responsibilities they carry. It would not be helpful to burden all coworkers with information that they know they should not have to bear. However, they have the right to know the answers to the questions, "Am I safe? Can I trust them?"

The generosity of recognition for years of service and excellence in workmanship also contributes to the overall sense of well-being within a work community and beyond. This reinforcement of "Every man is a piece of the continent"[49] is an essential affirmation of the community's

---

[49] "Poor Richard's Almanack – Benjamin Franklin Historical Society," n.d. http://www. benjamin-franklin-history.org/poor-richards-almanac/.

deeply held values. Responsibly recognizing the goodness and greatness of our colleagues, be it celebrating tenure, awards, or noteworthy contributions, affirms a sense of civility and respect within a work community. It provides an opportunity to continually restate the value of who we are and what we do. The impact of this recognition is not limited to the individuals being lauded within the work community. It extends to their family members, peer groups, clients, and vendor partners. Coworkers will likely share these affirmations around the dining room table, the Thanksgiving table, the classroom, and the backyard grill.

A curative culture seeks to provide generosity in much-needed and deserved vacation time. Balancing the needs of the individual with the needs of the work community requires wisdom and an understanding that rest and relaxation are restorative and should be encouraged.

Clearly articulated, equitable vacation policies are just

as significant as recognized holidays. Many coworkers link vacation time to holiday time to maximize their benefits. In a curative culture, coworkers not only obtain the necessary approvals for time off, but they also seek to coordinate with other members of their workgroup to cover the expectations of their position and the work community.

Caring leaders express their values in many ways. Vacations and holidays reflect a leader's beliefs about people, as do the quality of coverage in health benefits and paid sick and personal days. The level of excellence expected in the quality and quantity of work is better received by coworkers when reflected in the benefits provided. If you are in leadership at a nonprofit; keep reading, there are other avenues to express your generosity.

Financial generosity is the foundation upon which much of the above rests. Competitive salaries, raises, and bonuses are a necessity in a work community that expects excellence. Caring leaders understand this. They do not act entirely out of necessity, however. They seek thoughtful avenues to express financial appreciation because they take genuine delight in creatively expressing gratitude to those who exemplify greatness.

While financial generosity is foundational, it is not always easily practiced. For example, since nonprofit organizations utilize donor dollars to operate, a high degree of scrutiny is placed upon the cost of administration and fundraising. Despite this, caring nonprofit leaders know that there is no less need for financial generosity. Coworkers are still subject to the need for a fair wage like anyone else. They pay the same price for a gallon of gas as their for-profit counterparts. Experience indicates it is all a matter of scale. We know that few enter the nonprofit realm to amass wealth. Instead, they strive to accomplish their organization's mission. For the motivated nonprofit leader, there remains a vast array of ways to express generosity to coworkers. Creative retirement plans, extensive healthcare coverage, Flexible Spending Accounts, 403(b) accounts, housing allotments, and vehicle subsidies can provide many of the same expressions of gratitude that for-profit work communities accomplish through remuneration.

As we know, when work communities, either for-profit or nonprofit, are experiencing financial downturns, monetary generosity is difficult to achieve. Depending upon the nature and economic impact of their downturn, these work communities could see reductions in force, salary freezes, no cost-of-living increases or bonuses, and serious budget cuts. During these times, coworker commitments are tested as the work community shares in the financial constraints. At such moments, a community of generosity will more likely accommodate financial limitations with understanding and grace. Because generosity has been extended to them, the work community is better equipped to trust leaders who find it necessary to invoke budget-cutting measures.

Max De Pree's oldest child, Jody Vanderwel, tells the story of when her father faced tough financial times at the iconic furniture manufacturer, Herman Miller:

> "My mom was definitely my dad's best friend, his confidante and sounding board. One Sunday night, he told her the next day was going to be really hard. He was going to have to let several people go. And she said, "You're letting several families go." That led to more conversation and thinking. Ultimately, the company let the people in the plant vote on whether they would reduce headcount or reduce everyone's hours. The employees voted to reduce their hours and keep everybody employed."[50]

Coworkers in a work community represent much more than just themselves. As Max De Pree's wife, Esther, knew, coworkers really represent families.

On the brighter side, sometimes, in my mind's eye,

---

[50]Jonathan Becker, "The Magic of Max De Pree and Herman Miller: A Story From the Inside—This Team Works.," This Team Works., December 15, 2020, https://www. thisteamworks.com/blog/hermanmillerandmaxdepree.

I see a family gathered around the dinner table at night. By the look on Mom's and Dad's faces, something exciting is about to be announced. "Well, kids, I just received my bonus for the year, and today I made reservations for us all to go to… Disneyland!" The room erupts! The kids scream with delight and immediately begin declaring what rides they intend to make a priority.

There are other conversations around other tables, too. "Well, kids, I just received a raise, and it means we're finally going to be able to buy our own home!" or "We're going to fly to see grandma at Christmas!" or perhaps even, "We don't have to move after all!"

A community of generosity impacts every member of a work community personally and profoundly. While not a given, generosity begins the conversation that feeds a spirit of gratitude among coworkers.

13
A COMMUNITY OF GRATITUDE

We have explored the possible impact of the family of origin each coworker brings with them into the work community. This dynamic can also influence their ability and willingness to express gratitude. Some families hug, and others do not, some use words with great elocution while others use silence. Of course, there are many degrees of expression between these extremes, so it is with voicing gratitude.

As one would imagine, it is the leaders of a work community who set the tone for a community of gratitude. For some leaders, expressing gratitude within the work community comes as naturally as breathing. For this leader, everything and everyone is seen as a gift to the work community. Generally, this person understands that good events and good people are not simply "deserved" but instead are gifts to be celebrated.

Other leaders find expressing gratitude to be more of a challenge. While "positive reinforcement" is generally understood to be a force for good, it shouldn't be overdone. Many in this position have an underlying fear that too much praise can result in coworkers "letting up" in their work efforts. It's not inconsequential that this leader might feel uncomfortable both accepting praise and giving it. For this person, the concept of gratitude implies that somebody *gave* them something, which is true. For this leader, it is more acceptable to embrace a view that the good in their life is deserved and has come only as a direct result of their own intelligence and hard work.

Having worked for leaders who believe their position of leadership is deserved, I was also exposed to attitudes of high privilege reserved for what they perceived to be the "intellectually superior." I often heard employees and others who were deemed to be inferior referred to as "the unwashed masses." While extreme, this perspective can become the natural extension of those who perceive themselves to be self-made.

There are also those in leadership positions who recognize their hesitancy to embrace a posture of gratitude. They are, in fact, grateful, but full-on expressions of gratitude make them uncomfortable. For this leader, embracing something less emotional and perhaps humbler is easier. It is much more likely that this person might ascribe their good fortune to being "lucky."

There are certainly higher and lower degrees of each of these perspectives, which is evident in work communities as well. We humans are far too complex to be limited to just three viewpoints.

For most coworkers, embracing a community of gratitude requires more than a modicum of self-awareness.

There is a vulnerability in this that stems from a spirit of inquiry, both of themselves and those around them. The safety of a curative culture can provide the opportunity for open inquiry about who we are as human beings and our relationship to the community. A person who seeks to know more about gratitude and the possibility of embracing its benefits can find this opportunity in a curative culture.

In the cool spring mornings of island life in coastal Washington State, looking west, the gray of the sea melds into the slightly lighter gray of the clouds. The layers, like blankets, fold back in places, revealing glimpses of pale blue sky. Seagulls passing along the bluffs catch the light of the sun rising over the Cascade Mountains from the east. Their light gray bodies transform to the brightest white as the day crawls out of bed.

Further out on the water, black, birdlike forms become visible on the surface. Upon closer view, the rolling of dorsal fins reveals the passing pod of Orca whales on a morning hunt for salmon or seal. The silence of this moment, in itself, is a gift to the senses. Watching the world awaken is a gift.

Gratitude springs from highly sensitive powers of observation. It feels as though it comes to us when we allow ourselves to see with the eyes of the created, knowing what the Creator has made is indeed good.

My wife, Kathryn, and I frequently have breakfast at a café in town. One morning, the woman who is our server most days looked particularly spent. Kathryn leaned across the table and whispered, "She looks absolutely exhausted. How do you feel about leaving an extra-large tip for her today?" Glancing in her direction, I was quick to concur. Almost six months passed before our server paused at our table and told us about that day. It was a slow time at the restaurant, so she stopped by and told us what had caused her to be so very tired. "That was a very difficult day. I did not sleep at all the night before because my husband left me and told me he was going to get a divorce. I haven't said anything about it until now because I don't believe a person should bring their troubles into the workplace, but I just need to tell you," she said, with tears in her eyes, "what a lift it was for me to receive your gift that day. It helped me to realize that everything was going to be ok. And it is. Thank you so very much!" Kathryn had indeed had the eyes of the created that day.

One day, I received a call from my son, Graham, who is also the COO of our company, "Hell-o, I'm afraid I have some bad news…" He went on to relay that a woman in our company had just, very unexpectedly, lost her father and would need to take several days off. What I didn't know was that several of my employees had already sprung into action and established a Meal Train[51] for this coworker and

---

[51] "MealTrain.com (Official Site) - Organize Meal Support in Minutes," Meal Train, n.d., https://www.mealtrain.com/.

her family. This online service allowed members of our work community to sign up to provide meals during this time of family crisis. This caring act had highly impacted this grieving family. It also resulted in her profound gratitude at knowing that people from all across the company, living in several different states, had participated, even people that she didn't know very well. Perhaps Donne was right:

> No man is an island,
> Entire of itself,
> Every man is a piece of the continent,
> A part of the main.[52]

In a curative culture, seeing our work community as a gift right now, in the present, grants us the freedom to live with a sense of gratification in the moment. We can pause and be grateful now, rather than years later realizing "those really were the good old days." Even our most challenging relationships can have that moment when the morning sun

---

[52]Donne, *Devotions*

transforms them into the brightest white. Perhaps it can bring us comfort to know that those whom we frustrate can, maybe for a moment, see us in a positive light as well.

14
A COMMUNITY OF CIVILITY

Gratitude enhances our ability to recognize the humanity in our coworkers. In our best moments, it can evoke caring and kindness. In our less-than-best moments, civility can provide guardrails for our behavior when our better inclinations fail us.

If civility is courtesy and politeness[53], it doesn't appear to be a particularly high bar. Most socially capable coworkers do not find this challenging in their daily work life. Yet, as we know, there are times when civility seems to evade us, especially in times of extreme stress, frustration, or perceived provocation. Some days test our resolve, and sometimes we fail, as all humans do. On these fateful days, perhaps when our guard is down, we might lash out for a moment. We might say or write something that should not have been communicated.

[53]"Civility," in *Merriam-Webster Dictionary,* March 16, 2025, https://www.merriam-webster.com/dictionary/civility.

Regardless of the events leading up to this indiscretion, in this unfortunate circumstance, *we become the issue.*

Once we allow ourselves to become the issue, the situation has gotten out of hand. There is usually an outcry of "foul" that, regardless of the provocation's depth, frequency, or malintent, leaves the spotlight shining firmly upon us for our inappropriate communication. Once we, as leaders, become the issue, there is almost nothing we can say or do to put the focus back where we may feel it belongs. Experience teaches us that the only action left for us at this stage is to make a full, authentic, and proportionately public apology.

The mistake of lashing out exacerbates the situation, making things much worse than if we had said nothing at all. Our silence would not require an apology, nor would it set our agenda back in the way that becoming the issue tangles the line. Fortunately, the pain of becoming the issue is intense enough that it can be quite an effective teacher.

To those observing moments of incivility or civility, there is instruction as well. The ancient words, "A soft answer turns away wrath, but a harsh word stirs up anger,"[54] can induce respect for the one exhibiting restraint and erode trust in the one who becomes the issue. The modeling of civility helps to breathe health into the entire work community.

I had the privilege of working with the Senior Pastor of The First Presbyterian Church of Hollywood, Dr. Lloyd John Ogilvie, just before he became the 61st Chaplain of the U.S. Senate. Serving as a fundraising consultant to his broadcast ministry, *Let God Love You*, I spent many days in downtown Hollywood, California, in a small building just across the street from the church. It was here that I renewed my relationship with Inez Smith, who directed the ministry's operations.

I initially met Inez at Fuller Seminary, where she had served, for twenty years, as the Executive Administrative

[54]Proverbs 15:1, The Holy Bible (NIV)

Assistant to David Alan Hubbard, then President of Fuller Seminary. She also served as the President of the Pasadena City Women's Club, among her other civic duties.

Inez's brilliance was rivaled only by her poise. I greatly enjoyed revisiting our Fuller Seminary days over lunch. During one of those lunches, Inez relayed the story of how David Hubbard responded to his critics. She said, "When someone would write something horrid, criticizing David or the seminary, he would sit down and write a vigorous rebuttal. Once finished, he would hand it to me and say, 'Now file it, Inez.' He knew to respond in kind would be something he would later regret."

The same can be said of exercising grace in following a faux pas. It's quite impressive when a notable person responds to another person's faux pas with civility. The power of this behavior, offered by a person of great standing, is magnified many times over.

Shortly after Ronald Reagan left office in 1989, he moved his offices to the Fox Plaza building in Century City, California. It was best known as the set for the 1988 Bruce Willis film *Die Hard*. The morning I walked through the front door of this impressive structure, a Secret Service Agent sitting behind a desk greeted me. "Good morning, Mr. Shaw," he said. Taken aback that he knew my name, I quietly responded with, "G-Good M-Morning." The agent rose and escorted me to the elevator, using his special access card to push the penthouse button. I thanked him as the doors closed, leaving him behind.

As the elevator flew upward, I was filled with a mixture of excitement, anxiety, and total fascination. I experienced that foggy-tingly feeling in my mind that I have only known on the most important days of my life. Just meeting President Ronald Reagan would certainly have qualified as one of those days, but I was there for more than this. I was meeting my film crew in the Reagan Office Complex to record television and radio public service announcements by "The Great Communicator" himself!

As the elevator doors opened, I was confronted with a large white marble bust of George Washington and a bowl of Jelly Belly® jellybeans, known to be President Reagan's favorite candy throughout his political career.[55] My public relations consultant was waiting there in the hallway, and he quickly ushered me into the conference room attached to the Reagan offices. There, I met up with the film crew, who had arrived early to set up and test their equipment before recording.

Once we had greeted each other, we met President Reagan's publicist. She was giving us our instructions, when the door opened and two Secret Service agents stepped inside and out of the way of President Reagan, who walked into the room talking, laughing, and putting on his suit

---

[55]"Jelly Belly® Jelly Beans and Ronald Reagan," Ronald Reagan, n.d., https://www. reaganlibrary.gov/reagans/ronald-reagan/jelly-bellyr-jelly-beans-and-ronald-reagan.

coat. He made the rounds of everyone in the room, shaking hands and making conversation. He was very relaxed, told a few jokes, and then we went to work.

I'm certain my voice quivered as I gave instructions to the President, telling him we were doing both television and radio spots to celebrate the 100th anniversary of the revered Union Rescue Mission of Los Angeles. I motioned toward the teleprompter and indicated that we could begin whenever he was ready. Sitting in his designated chair, he nodded to the cameraman and then launched into a perfect teleprompter reading of endorsement and congratulations to Union Rescue Mission. When he was finished, he looked up at me as if to say, "Okay?" I turned to the production director, and he said, "Let's do one more take, okay?" Looking back to President Reagan, I conveyed the message. He sat there, gave me a brief look that I read as, "Really? You've got to be kidding me?" then, with great civility, he turned to the teleprompter and did the second take.

Ronald Reagan didn't need to set aside time to meet with us. He certainly had done enough public service in his life and had earned his ease. But he chose to do the endorsement, and, as I learned years later while reading a book written by one of his Secret Service Agents,[56] this great man was well-known for and took pride in his "first-take" capabilities while recording. He had humored our little crew's faux pas with his civility.

Courtesy and politeness are cherished values in a curative culture. Coworkers find they can enjoy the fresh breeze of civility as they step away from a toxic workplace.

---

[56]John R. Barletta and Rochelle Schweizer, Riding With Reagan: From the White House to the Ranch (Citadel, 2017).

15

A COMMUNITY OF HONESTY

If one of the fundamental questions coworkers have regarding their colleagues and work community is, "Can I trust them?" then how should they be answered?

In this context, trust implies a sustained level of fulfilled expectations. We place our trust in those who act and speak appropriately and predictably, reflecting our shared values and expectations. Trust results from an established pattern of predictable honesty in the words, behavior, and character of a curative work community.

In this community of honesty, which is understood as meaning "adherence to the facts,"[57] coworkers find fidelity to reality. What they see, hear, and experience in their work community squares with what they know to be true. In this prevailing wind of security, coworkers are free to

---

[57] "Honesty," in *Merriam-Webster Dictionary*, March 13, 2025, https://www.merriam-webster.com/dictionary/honesty.

be less distracted by speculation and ill motives.

Honesty is best preserved when battles for truth are fought up front. There are those within the work community and those being served by them, customers, if you will, who deeply *want something to be true* that is not. The pressure in these moments leads many to appease the force coming to bear upon them. The strain of standing up to those using their position to *will* something into reality creates a tension that is difficult to hold at bay and redirect. But sadly, there is no reward for submission.

Many years ago, before I had my own company, I worked for an agency that often struggled with honesty. They were not pathological in their deception, but often, when pressure came from clients to raise more money than our company had projected, they would relent and modify our income projections to please the client in the moment. On one occasion, my client service team had carefully studied the numbers, worked long and hard to maximize direct-mail income, and incorporated the higher costs the company's owners provided to us. The resulting income forecast left us showing very little growth in net income. I knew it would be a hard sell to our client, but I just couldn't justify a higher income forecast to offset our company's higher prices. The owners were not pleased when I presented my team's work to them. They challenged my team's income figures. We returned to our offices to double-check our work and returned with very little improvement in our client's bottom line. One of the owners took my income forecast from me and, with a red pen, revised our projections upward by almost 1 million dollars! He handed the revised document back to me. Glaring, he said, "Here's what we are giving to the client, and you'll support these numbers when we're presenting them!" I nodded, took the marked-up document, and adjusted our presentation accordingly. I also took the liberty of filing the marked-up copy in a secure location should I need to produce it in the future. Such was the level of distrust in the leadership of that company.

The following week, the owners and my team flew to Los Angeles to make our presentation. It was, on the surface, a very congenial meeting. Everyone was happy. The owners were pleased with our client's increased spend, the client was pleased with the promise of the additional income they needed for the next fiscal year, and I was happy that I had not come across as disloyal to the company's owners. In the short term, all was right with the world.

On the flight home from Los Angeles to Dallas, I felt a deep sense of conflict. I knew my original income projections were as accurate as I could make them. I also recalled the red markings all over my work by one of the owners and the fierce look in his eyes as he instructed me to make his revisions. But there was another look that now haunted me. It was the trusting eyes of the CEO of the organization we had just left, having assured him our numbers were solid. I vowed to myself that, should I ever be an owner, I would never force my team to inflate income projections to be able to make more profit or to please a client.

There was no winner in this act of straying from the truth. Our client's income continued to fall short of the inflated forecast. After being summoned back to L.A. to address the situation, the income forecast was lowered to more realistic levels, our clients spend with our agency was reduced, and the client's trust in the company was significantly eroded. My own confidence in the honesty of the owners dropped through the floor.

Those who believe they can simply *will* something to be true are also often afflicted with selective memory. In the end, your acquiescence to their will has somehow become your idea rather than theirs. Therefore, experience teaches it is best to redirect wishful thinking back into the realm of reality at the very outset. It is far better to be known for holding fast to your understanding of reality, however disagreeable, at the very moment the idea is introduced than to be accused of being misleading or unsuccessful after expectations have fallen short. "If you knew it wasn't possible, you should have told me" are words that can only be preempted if the battle is fought up front. Granted, none of this is easy. We would do well to reflect upon our own moments of exerted will or acquiescence lest we judge the appeaser too harshly.

Fear of conflict leads many of us down this path of regret. Perhaps it's helpful to embrace the reality inherent in knowing that the fear of conflict that leads us to acquiescence will not prevent the conflict; it will merely postpone it. It's quite possible the toll of delay is greater than facing the conflict as it arises. Experience indicates that facing the conflict early on is much less stressful over time and, in the end, less frightening than we might imagine.

Honesty requires a commitment to factuality. Knowing what is real requires a dedication to the laborious process of discovering the truth of a situation, fact-checking, if you will. The amount of effort expended is seldom regretted, however, as it arms the espouser with all the minute details necessary to support the truth of a reality-based perspective.

Guessing at the truth seems perilously close to conveying an untruth. In a community of honesty, there exists a commitment to not guess. Is a project going to be on time? Talk to the various parties involved. Will quality have to be sacrificed to achieve the deadline? The people involved can tell you. Are the Key Performance Indicators going to be met? Asking the right questions of the right people can provide the information necessary. In a culture of honesty, coworkers are not afraid to work hard to determine reality. They also understand there is no penalty for saying, "I don't know, but I'll know more in a week." As leaders, it is critical that we affirm the messenger and embrace reality when it is presented to us.

Some make the distinction between "white lies" and "lies." Generally, it's held that the former are told about something inconsequential to avoid hurting another person.[58] The latter involves the intent to deceive. Unfortunately, any kind of lie can be discovered. Once this has happened, the ability to distinguish between them diminishes greatly. One might argue that telling white lies makes it all the easier to engage in deception. The result of either lie is broken trust. In a culture of honesty, any kind of untruth is avoided.

When a coworker asks the question, "Can I trust them?" it can mean so much more than "Do they lie to me?" It is also a question about fairness and straightforwardness within the work community. This question leads us to an understanding of integrity in a curative culture.

---

[58]"Lie," in Merriam-Webster Dictionary, n.d., https://www.merriam-webster.com/dictionary/lie.

16
A COMMUNITY OF INTEGRITY

Diogenes, the ancient Greek philosopher, was actually born in Sinope, Turkey.[59] Arriving in Athens, he couldn't find affordable housing, leading him to take shelter in an old wooden barrel that lay on its side in the marketplace. Today, he is best known for having carried a lamp through the streets of Athens "in search of an honest man." Diogenes was embraced by the populace because he spoke his mind without any formality or filter. He was seen as someone who would say what he thought to be true without regard for a person's feelings or social status. In so doing he was seen by many as having integrity or being incorruptible, a man of the people.

For our purposes, it might be more useful to look again to creation when seeking a model of integrity or incorruptibility. The Olympic range of mountains stands

---

[59]The Editors of Encyclopaedia Britannica, "Diogenes | Biography, Philosophy, & Facts," Encyclopedia Britannica, March 18, 1999, https://www.britannica.com/biography/Diogenes-Greek-philosopher.

on a vast peninsula between Seattle and the Pacific Ocean. It seems to be arranged perfectly, shielding most of Puget Sound from a direct onslaught by the winter storms forming to the west over the open sea.

Coastal communities such as Forks, Washington, average over 119 inches of rainfall per year.[60] Because of the heavy shield of the Olympic range, Seattle, well known for its rain, receives 37.13 inches of precipitation annually on average.[78] Compare this with Vancouver, British Columbia, 136 miles to the north. Without the buffer of the Olympics, this great Canadian city receives 57.3 inches.[61]

This Olympic shield has 471 prominences with 244 named mountains, the tallest of which is Mount Olympus, standing at 7,890 feet. This powerful peninsular upheaval of rock, earth, and forest evokes expressions of wonder and awe. When snow-covered, their definition reflects the morning sun

[60]"Weather Averages Forks, Washington," US Climate Data, n.d., https://www.usclimatedata.com/climate/forks/washington/united-states/uswa0149.

[61]"Average Yearly Precipitation in Canadian Cities - Current Results," n.d., https://www.currentresults.com/Weather/Canada/Cities/precipitation-annual-average.php.

onto the mainland in a crisp whiteness matched only by the bright sails of those who, in their boats, venture out in the morning light on the saltwater from which these peaks ascend. At sunset, the sky makes a unique presentation every evening and backlights their darkening slopes with its colors.

Within the northern end of the range, there is what appears to be the profile of a man lying on his back, looking upward to the heavens. He was there, doing his duty, shielding the Sound, or the "Whulge"[62] as the Native peoples called it, a word which mimics the sound of the gentle surf as they traveled the crystal-clear waters in their cedar canoes. He was there in 1792 when Captain George Vancouver first sailed past him into the Strait of Juan de Fuca and renamed the Whulge, Puget Sound, after Peter Puget, one of his officers. The man in the mountains is there today without wavering as a reminder to us all to look up to creation for examples of integrity.

---

[62]David B. Williams, *Homewaters: A Human and Natural History of Puget Sound*, 2022.

Integrity doesn't change as the generations pass. It rises above, shielding those who need to know there is good in the world from those with less honorable intent.

A culture of integrity doesn't have to remember what promises were made 300 years ago, 10 years ago, or even yesterday. Adherence to a moral code that represents reality to one another keeps the air clean of deceptions, manipulations, and innuendos. Each day then is a new opportunity to focus on the rigors of solving problems and pursuing opportunities that inevitably face every work community.

Manifestations of integrity in the work community serve as a binding force that provides opportunities for coworkers to interact with each other, knowing that things are as they appear to be. Exhibiting integrity is the most impactful answer to the question, "Am I safe?"

A curative culture stands on the shoulders of comm-

itments that are expected to be kept. For members of a curative work community, this is not a hope; it's a proven principle. It's proven by competent, caring leadership that says what
it means and means what it says. It's proven when the entire
DNA of the company exudes incorruptibility. When coworkers know and expect a sense of fairness to prevail when conflicts arise, it is a constant reminder that in this place of business, disruption and deception will not be tolerated.

The level of trust in evidence at all elevations of
a curative work community satisfies both a longing for
honesty and a respectful sense of optimism that such a
work community might actually exist. Integrity encap-
sulates a magnetic quality that attracts the soul in a manner
much akin to the concept of freedom.

The attraction of experiencing integrity is faith-build-
ing. For people who have had their faith in humanity battered or their belief in leadership severely shaken, integrity

can become the siren's song. Integrity woos the hungry heart. Its curative nature can help to bind up the wounds accumulated in the brambles of toxicity.

The confidence built in the presence of incorruptibility is not only restorative; it is transmittable. If carefully tended, the pollen of integrity will permeate the many ecosystems within a work community. It is life-enhancing in its nature and restorative to those seeking a respite from a toxic work environment.

There will always be challenges to our integrity, perhaps the most common being money, followed closely by fame and power. While none of these symbols of success are intrinsically corrupting, few would debate the potential for an insidious imbalance to occur. Headlines and history are replete with the stories of those who have not met this challenge well. One of the most memorable examples of corruption is the Enron scandal. When it occurred, I had been traveling to Houston for years and remembered hearing people speak of this high-profile energy trading company with reverence and awe. The founder, Ken Lay, was known for his philanthropic contributions to one of the nonprofits I served there. With the onset of Congressional de-regulation in the early 1990s, Enron lost its competitive edge and began to see the massive profit base it enjoyed plummet. Jeffrey Skilling, a consultant who was eventually hired as the company's COO, initiated a significant culture shift to emphasize aggressive trading and, together with one of his recruits, Andrew Fastow, who became the CFO, began complex and fraudulent accounting practices to give the appearance of meteoric profitability. At the same time, Enron moved closer and closer to filing bankruptcy. Its accounting firm and consultant, Arthur Andersen, was accused of shredding Enron-related documents. Many Enron executives were found guilty and sentenced to prison. Ken Lay and Jeffrey

Skilling were both found guilty of conspiracy and fraud. Lay died before entering prison on a 45-year sentence, and Skilling served 12 years of his own 24-year sentence.[63]

I remember driving past Enron Field on Crawford Street, home to the Houston Astros, and seeing the marks where the Enron logo had been removed the night before. Media helicopters were circling the stadium, carrying the stories of Enron's failure to operate with integrity.

There are also certainly those who have met the challenges of accumulating wealth with impressive strength. Who among us hasn't heard the expression, "You know, money hasn't changed him at all." This phrase is usually an expression of admiration and appreciation for the values of the person who can maintain their equilibrium amid the pressures of these corrupting influences. The rarity of this ability to hold fast to deeply held values in the presence of realized dreams is testimony to the value of being incorruptible, or, in other

---

[63]Bondarenko and Peter, "Enron Scandal | Summary, Explained, History, & Facts," Encyclopedia Britannica, February 3, 2025, https://www.britannica.com/event/Enron-scandal.

words, having integrity. A curative culture cannot exist without the realized presence of this indispensable attribute.

17
A COMMUNITY OF PROMISES KEPT

In a curative culture, promises are made, remembered, and, within the bounds of reality, they are kept. It's understood that reality is an active ingredient in a work community's ability to fulfill its promises. When keeping promises is the norm, a foundation of trust becomes a deeply rooted characteristic of the culture. It strengthens the resolve of the work community and allows it to stand firm in the face of adversity.

The Great Recession of 2007-2009 tested the resolve of many work communities. Jobs were lost, promotions were delayed or canceled, and bonuses were largely nonexistent. As a company owner, answering my phone became a difficult task. It felt like every time a client called, it was to cancel their contract. Donors were giving less and less often. Our clients either attempted to do their own direct response fundraising or turned to less expensive, less donor-friendly services. Those of us in leadership positions were finding it increasingly difficult to keep our financial commitments to our work community. The realities of the savings and loan debacle left many financial institutions in untenable positions. And the impact of these market forces lingered for many more years, making it difficult for businesses to gain access to capital. That was just the reality.

The good news about a work community that lives in reality is that coworkers can be counted on to weather the bad times and the good. This is especially true when leadership sacrifices first. Larger salaried coworkers can absorb salary freezes or, if necessary, salary cuts when times are particularly tough. Reducing income for those with significantly lower salaries is much more difficult. Times such as the Great Recession required many owners to put money into their companies rather than extract profits from them. Surviving in a very difficult economic environment makes it even more understandable that the very existence of the work community is an implied promise of vigilant and proactive leadership.

Salaries in themselves are a promise made. The recipient promises to earn the amount committed to them, and the company promises to be faithful in prioritizing and honoring paydays. Expense reports are quickly reimbursed because the money is spent on the work community's behalf, and the coworker's cash flow is no less important than the company's.

It must be said that promises within a curative work community extend well beyond remuneration. They extend to the promise of a respectful work environment and a culture of truth, caring, and encouragement.

Every member in a curative work culture is promised to be given the resources to face the day, knowing they are positioned to achieve excellence. They know what is expected of them. They have been well-trained for their position, and they know when they have achieved the desired outcome. They also know they are not expected to be flawless or perfect.

This promise of resources implies the safety net of recovery when mistakes are made. Every coworker's vigilance helps to braid the strands of this net. There is a promise of helping each other succeed that rises above other agendas. "How can I help?" is not a social question. It is a sincere offer to help solve each other's problems and correct each other's mistakes. It's understood that this is not an offer to do a coworker's job for them; neither is it habitual covering for inattentiveness or lack of caring. It is the awareness that, from time to time, we all need another set of eyes, another perspective, or another set of hands to help us correct a misstep.

Achieving excellence implies the promise of proper

training for those entering the work community or those ascending or transitioning to new responsibilities. The very definition of training, "the skill, knowledge, or experience acquired by one that trains,"[64] provides perspective. A coworker who is training for a new or modified set of responsibilities brings their best self to a learning process administered by those who have already attained proficiency.

Those committed to becoming trainers usually assume added responsibilities in providing this service. There is a higher level of responsibility in assuming this role. The trainer is most likely expected to cover their own workload and provide tutelage to the trainee.

The person assuming this responsibility must ask themselves critical questions. Perhaps the first being, "Do I have mastery over my subject?" followed by, "Am I aware of and agreeing to the extra work required?" "Am I committed to making myself accessible to the trainee?" "Have

---

[64]"Training," in Merriam-Webster Dictionary, March 12, 2025, https://www.merriam-webster.com/dictionary/training.

I invested myself in understanding how the trainee best learns?" "Am I willing to invest myself in assuring their success?" The implied promises in these questions can provide the secure underpinnings of the work community itself.

A curative work community understands that co-workers depend upon implicit and explicit promises that are made and kept. The keeping of these promises that helps to heal the work wounds we all carry and contributes to the answers to the questions we all ask: "Can I trust them and their intentions?" "Are they worthy of my respect?" "Am I safe?"

18
A COMMUNITY OF IMPACT

For those who remember their history, Thailand was the primary refuge for those stumbling out of "the killing fields"[65] where the Khmer Rouge, under the control of Pol Pot, had systematically slaughtered 1.3 million people between 1975 and 1979. Some have referred to this genocide as "the Auschwitz of Asia."

When the men, women, and children who had managed to survive the carnage fell across the border into Thailand, many humanitarian organizations were waiting to help. World Relief, my employer at the time, administrated a border hospital there called Sakeao, which was the name of the province where it was located. I was sent there, with a photographer, to become educated on the herculean efforts of the international humanitarian relief community and ob-

---

[65]"The Killing Fields (1984) " IMDb, February 1, 1985, https://www.imdb.com/title/tt0087553/.

tain photos and stories to share with donors back in the United States.

The Vietnamese Army, who we knew as the Viet Cong, invaded Cambodia and put an end to Pol Pot's reign of terror. But the country was decimated. What little food remained was being consumed by the occupying troops. The survivors of the work camps and slaughter of the Pol Pot regime were starving to death.

The international community began moving massive shipments of rice to the border between Cambodia and Thailand, some of it at a place in the Aranyaprathet district called Nong Chan. Those who were able brought their wooden-wheeled oxcarts to the border from inside Cambodia in the hope of transporting this life-sustaining rice back to their families and villages. A high-impact plan, had it not been for the Vietnamese army that intercepted the oxcarts just inside the jungles as the Cambodians left the border to return home. The international community was unintentionally feeding the Vietnamese Army.

By the time I arrived in Nong Chan, the aid community, funded largely by western governments working through nonprofit aid agencies, had developed a workaround they called "The Land Bridge." Rather than sending food rice back into the jungles of Cambodia just to be intercepted, they began sending seed rice, which the Cambodian populace could plant with the hope they would be able to use some to sustain themselves before the Vietnamese army confiscated the rest.

It proved to be an effective plan. The seed rice was making its way into the villages of this ravaged country. But two unforeseen issues were diminishing its progress. The wooden oxcarts had wooden axles that were worn out and kept breaking under the loads of rice seed. To make matters worse, the oxen who pulled them were diseased and dying.

I had been taken to the border by two enterprising World Relief workers who fancied themselves as "the border cowboys." In their small Toyota pickup, they would traverse back and forth across the opening in the jungle at Nong Chan, monitoring an operation I can only describe as ingenious and highly dangerous.

Arriving at a deep waterfilled ditch, the cowboys stopped the pickup and asked, "You want to go to Cambodia?" Caught up in their enthusiasm and not fully understanding the implications, should I have been captured by the Vietnamese, the remaining Khmer Rouge, or the Khmer Siri, who all milled about holding AK-47s and many with rifle rocket-packs on their backs, I responded, "Yeah, let's go for it!" With that, one of the cowboys jammed the Toyota in gear and began traversing the ditch on two very uninspiring planks that bowed low toward the water as we rolled across the ditch into one of the most tortured countries in modern history.

This was all happening under the watchful eye of the Thai soldiers who "stood guard" on their side of the ditch. Most of them couldn't have been more than 19, and many held an AK-47 in one hand and a bottle of Johnny Walker Red in the other. One took a long pull out of his bottle as we rolled past him. "Don't look directly at him, and NO photographs," counseled one of the cowboys, "They have total authority out here and shoot somebody every few days just to show they're in charge."

Once safely across the ditch, we drove out into a large clearing. The operation consisted of a small, toll-booth-sized shack where a diminutive gentleman dressed in a rubber apron and tall rubber boots was undertaking a highly hazardous task. He would emerge from the shack holding a foot-long syringe filled with green liquid. The business end of the syringe held the largest needle I had ever seen. Adjusting the syringe, he would slowly approach an unsuspecting ox, walking backwards he put his foot on its hindquarters, and, holding the syringe in one hand, he would slam the huge needle through its thick hide. His other hand pushed the vaccine in as quickly as possible before the ox would bellow and kick him about 6 feet away! Landing on his face in the mud, he'd get his knees under him and stand back up, ready to receive his next victim from the long line of oxcarts waiting. Impressed with the veterinarian's courage, one of the cowboys marveled, "He does this all day, every day."

Another operation was occurring right next to the shack. It involved removing the worn wooden axles from the oxcarts and replacing them with shiny new steel. The weight of the rice seed would now be transferred to the wheels, which were also being replaced with new steel rims, making them last much longer.

Here, in this opening in the jungle on the border between Cambodia and Thailand, lay much of the hope of feeding the people of Cambodia. The impact of The Land Bridge was tremendous, given that aid agencies estimated that 2.5 million[66] people were at risk of starvation during this time. The occupying forces of Vietnam did not confiscate the oxcarts returning inside the country bearing seed rice. They needed the Cambodian people to plant, tend, and harvest the rice. Reportedly, Cambodia had a bumper crop of rice the following harvest.[67]

The impact of committed people who know what to do, have the resources they need, and are willing to innovate as circumstances dictate can literally change the world for good.

A culture of impact is a work community that understands why they labor. Assuming the need for remuneration is a given, coworkers who seek to understand the result

---

[66]Arthur Defehr, "Landbridge– a Personal Perspective," August 30, 2005, https://artdefehr.com/documents/bl012-a-050930landbridgeand-cambodia1.pdf.
[67]Defehr, *Landbridge*

of what they are helping to accomplish are highly motivated. Far more than being just a job, they share in the values that are reflected to them in the eyes of their impactful coworkers. In so doing they gain a sense of fulfillment that further bonds them to their work community.

It is incumbent that the leadership of a work community leads the way in this endeavor. A leader who exerts awareness and energy to instill a deep understanding of impact will be rewarded with immense commitment from the work community. Understanding, shared values, and commitment drive a culture of excellence to achieve maximum effort.

When a standard of excellence permeates a work community, it enhances the communal sense of significance, inspiring a self-propelled workplace culture of the highest sort. The thrill of working beside others who share in this respect for accomplishment has very few rivals. It's extraordinarily rare to have the privilege of belonging to a team of highly talented individuals who are committed to improving humanity with their labor. Some may ask, "How often does this really happen?" I can only respond that a curative culture is not only possible; it already exists when we as leaders see our coworkers as living, breathing people with families who depend on them and not merely a replaceable resource to accomplish our business goals. Building a curative culture of significant impact requires intentionality. "If it was easy, anybody could do it!"

19
A COMMUNITY OF HUMILITY

"When pride comes, then comes disgrace,
but with humility comes wisdom."
— **Proverbs 11:2 NIV**

Even though the passage cited above is from the Bible, one need not be religious to appreciate humility in others. It's an attractive trait to most of us. Refreshing in its discovery, it may well be an indicator of how seldom it is encountered in our day-to-day interactions.

Humility, defined as "freedom from pride or arrogance: the quality or state of being humble,"[68] has a vine-ripened flavor attractive to most. That is not to say we ourselves exhibit humility most of the time, but when we encounter it, its endearing quality moves us in ways that remind us of the incredibly inviting approachability

---

[68]"Humility," in *Merriam-Webster Dictionary*, March 14, 2025, https://www.merriam-webster.com/dictionary/humility.

it engenders.

In a curative culture, humility's presence creates a longing for extended exposure. Usually found in coworkers who quietly go about their day, this soothing quality emanates from their presence, in the words they speak, and the actions they embody.

There is an ancient quality to humility that is as healing as walking on the softness of a moss-covered forest floor. Many have been heard to use the phrase "old soul" following a pleasant interaction with a person exhibiting this healing quality in their personality. Encounters with old souls leave us feeling like we have connected with someone who has lived longer than their years. They exhibit a small window into past decades, centuries, or even millennia. Often, old souls speak simple truths in soft voices. For this reason, it's easy to pass them by for those who speak loudly. And they don't seem to be bothered if they're not heard the first time they speak to a subject. It's like they know the loud ones come and go. Their turn to be heard will come; everything in its own good time. History tends to come down on their side.

Part of the lure of traveling to places like the Great Pyramids of Egypt, the Great Wall of China, the Coliseum in Rome and for people of faith, the Holy Land, is the opportunity to reach out and touch a piece of human history. Walking where the ancients lived, worked, and related to each other holds a deep primordial majesty that touches our souls with the comfort of the human experience. Physical evidence of past mistakes and triumphs and well-worn words of archaic wisdom serve to enlighten our own journey.

I have been fortunate to experience rare moments of walking where the ancients once walked. One of my favorite adventures was a flyfishing excursion to western British Columbia, specifically the Insular Mountains on Vancouver Island. My guide led me to the heart of those emerald mountains via a forest path that was about 18 inches wide and worn almost two feet deep. The trail was shrouded in moss and appeared to be virtually untouched by the centuries. The Nuu-chah-nulth peoples of western Vancouver Island created this footpath while traveling overland to trade with tribes on the eastern side of the Island and the mainland beyond. I felt humbled to walk where people who had lived so long ago had left the literal imprint of their life's journeys worn into the earth. I wondered how many footsteps it would have taken, and over how many centuries or millennia to leave this evidence etched into the mountains.

There is a humility that comes from the realization of our place in time. Our own moment is just that, a moment, a mere period in the sentences of the stories of the human experience.

I find it inspiring that in many cultures, including those of the Native peoples of the Pacific Northwest, elders were and are revered. The honor and respect afforded the elders is old-soul behavior at its finest. It seems that it is the ancient informing the culture of today.

As we know, there is so much to learn about life in a work community. In a curative culture, humility is prized for its seasoning of the whole. Respect, the birthplace of humility, guides the work community in its reverence for the elders. Older and wiser coworkers who remain embedded within the work community or choose to come alongside it, offer perspectives, experiences, and insights that are not yet available to those who have not traveled as far.

Embracing the elders in a work community proves professional discipline. Words like *change, progress,* and *innovation* have always been and always will be with us. With our elders, it will not be so. In the not-too-distant future, there will come a time when the elders in our lives will all have moved on, and the realization will begin to settle in: "I am now an elder." The ancient voice of Job comes to mind,

> "But ask the animals, and they will teach you,
> Or the birds of the air, and they will tell you;
> Or speak to the earth, and it will teach you,
> Or let the fish of the sea inform you.
> Which of all these does not know that
> the hand of the Lord has done this?
> In his hand is the life of every creature
> And the breath of all mankind.
> Does not the ear test words
> as the tongue tastes food?
> Is not wisdom found among the aged?
> Does not long life bring understanding?"[69]

To embrace the ancient does not require the abandonment of the future. There is discipline in understanding change, progress, and innovation within the context of the wisdom of the elders. Humility is the gift of not being threatened by the knowledge, experience, and expertise of others. Humility regards others as greater than ourselves. It prepares us to *interpret* change, to *define* meaningful progress, and helps us to *prioritize* the innovation needed to move our

---

[69]Job 12:7-12, The Holy Bible (NIV)

work community forward. It requires humility to seek the wisdom of the elders, but the journey is worth the effort!

CONCLUSION

When one of the old giants releases its hold on the forest floor and comes crashing down, it doesn't say goodbye to the earth. The ancient trees, once rising tall, reaching up to the heavens for centuries or even millennia, who drew their sustenance from the soil, provided cover for wildlife and shade for the undergrowth, will all, eventually, become the earth itself. So it is, so it has been since the beginning when the Creator spoke, it was so.

In nature, these magnificent pillars of life simply become another source of nutrients to those trees who yet live. Resting on the earth, they become "nurse logs" for the seedlings whose beginnings fall from those left standing. In many ways, nature itself is a curative culture if not interfered with by the toxic practices of man.

Nature provides a source of comfort that woos city dwellers into making pilgrimages to the countryside on the weekends, vacations, and holidays. The summer home, the lake house, a place at the shore, or maybe just a room with a view sing to the soul in a way that nothing man-made can ever achieve.

To those fortunate enough to live a rural life, there are occasional forays into the cities. The stark contrasts there leave many rural dwellers wondering at the source of its attraction. Living rural early on in my life was both a gift and an agitation. The former was a compass I carried with me deep in my chest, and the latter brought a sense of alienation from my urban and suburban surroundings.

To hear the calling of nature's voice in one's life is a gift to the soul. It need not come, as it did for me, in childhood. It can arrive at any time and in any place. You can hear and feel the longing for the peace found only in nature in the words to this beautiful urban song:

> When this old world starts getting me down
> And people are just too much for me to face
> I climb way up to the top of the stairs
> And all my cares just drift right into space

> On the roof its peaceful as can be
> And there the world below can't bother me
> Let me tell you now

> When I come home feeling tired and beat
> I go up where the air is fresh and sweet
> I get away from the hustle and crowds
> And all that rat race noise down in the street

> On the roof's the only place I know
> Where you just have to wish to make it so
> Oh, let's go up on the roof

> At night the stars put on a show for free
> And, darling, you can share it all with me
> Keep on telling you

> Right smack dab in the middle of town
> I found a paradise that's trouble-proof
> So if this world starts getting you down

There's room enough for two, up on the roof
Up on the roof, everything is all right
Up on the roof, oh, come on, baby

Up on the roof
Everything is all right
Up on the roof[70]

The relationship between nature and a curative culture is forever intertwined with the concept of *imago dei,* the image of God. This concept is familiar to many Native or Indigenous brothers and sisters. If we believe the Creator provided us with this pristine globe, as many of them do, Mother Earth, the blue marvel of the solar system, then perhaps we can take hope in the concept of the curative aspects of nature. If toxicity is diminished or removed, the natural tendency is for the Earth to heal itself.

So it is in our relationships with each other. When we bring ourselves into our workplace, our footprints combine with those of our coworkers, creating our work culture.

---

[70]"Up on the Roof" by Carole King and Gerry Goffin, produced by Leiber and Stoller, Atlantic Records, released as a single on September 17, 1962.

Caring leaders and coworkers know the power of life-giving values and the vigilance required to call us back to them. The result is a curative culture that breathes "fresh and sweet" air into the work community, and the stars will "put on a show for free."

BIBLIOGRAPHY

Aviation Oil Outlet. "The Early History of Commercial Air Travel." May 3, 2017. https://aviationoiloutlet.com/blog/early-history-commercial-air-travel/?srsltid=AfmBOopgaGgBUHoFYvSYAl9NKnpkASHmBDLAX6ZsfxuqzeywqtX56If3

Barletta, John R., Schweizer, Rochelle. *Riding With Reagan, from the White House to the Ranch.* Citadel Press, 2005

Benjamin Franklin Historical Society. "Poor Richard's Almanac." http://www.benjamin-franklin-history.org/poor-richards-almanac/

Becker, Jonathan. "The Magic of Max De Pree and Herman Miller: A Story from the Inside." Weblog. This Team Works. (blog), December 15, 2020. https://www.thisteamworks.com/blog/hermanmillerandmaxdepree.

Britannica. "A Christmas Carol, by Charles Dickens." Last Updated: Feb. 4, 2025. https://www.britannica.com/topic/A-Christmas-Carol-novel

Britannica. "Diogenes." Updated January 14, 2025. https://www.britannica.com/biography/Diogenes-Greek-philosopher

Britannica. "Enron Scandal, United States History." Last updated February 3, 2025. https://www.britannica.com/event/Enron-scandal

Britannica. "Philip Stanhope, 4th Earl of Chesterfield."
February 22, 2024. https://www.britannica.com/
biography/Philip-Stanhope-4th-Earl-of-Chesterfield

Brown, Colin, ED. *The New International Dictionary of New
Testament Theology, vol.2*. Zondervan Publishing Company,
1981.

Bureau of Labor Statistics. "Employee Tenure in 2024." https://
www.bls.gov/news.release/pdf/tenure.pdf.

Busby, Dean M., and Emilie Iliff. "The Impact of Family
of Origin Experiences." In *Routledge eBooks*, 134–43, 2017.
https://doi.org/10.4324/9781315678610-14.

CNBC. "Charlie Munger, investing genius and Warren
Buffett's right-hand man, dies at age 99." Updated
Wed, Nov 29 20237:51 AM EST. https://www.cnbc.
com/2023/11/28/charlie-munger-investing-sage-and-
warren-buffetts-confidant-dies.html

Current Results. "Average Annual Precipitation for Canadian
Cities." Accessed March 13, 2025. https://www.
currentresults.com/Weather/Canada/Cities/precipitation-
annual-average.php

DeFehr, Arthur. "Landbridge, A Personal Perspective."
September 30, 2005. https://artdefehr.com/documents/
bl012-a-050930landbridgeand-cambodia1.pdf

De Pree, Max. *Leadership is an Art*. Crown Business, 2004.

De Pree, Max. *Leadership is an Art*. Michigan State University
Press, 1987.

Dickens, Charles. *A Christmas Carol.* Chapman & Hall, 1843.

Donald, David Herbert. *Lincoln.* Simon & Schuster, 1996.

Donne, John, 1572-1631. *Devotions upon Emergent Occasions.* The University Press, 1923.

Federal Reserve History. "The Great Depression." Written as of November 22, 2013. https://www.federalreservehistory. org/essays/great-depression

Greenleaf, Robert K. *Servant Leadership, A Journey into the Nature of Legitimate Power & Greatness.* Paulist Press, 1977.

Greenleaf, Robert K. *25ᵗʰ Anniversary Edition of Servant Leadership, A Journey into the Nature of Legitimate Power & Greatness.* Paulist Press, 1977.

History of Information. "In His "Meditationes Sacrae" Francis Bacon Writes "Ipsa Scientia Potestas Est" (Knowledge is Power)." https://www.historyofinformation. com/detail.php?id=5253

IMDb. "The Killing Fields." Release date November 2, 1984. https://www.imdb.com/title/tt0087553/

Investopedia. "10 Years After the Financial Crisis: The Impact on Small Business." Updated February 27, 2023. https:// www.investopedia.com/small-business/10-years-after-financial-crisis-impact-small-business/

Jason Downs. "25 Metaphors for Nature". August 26, 2024. https://idiominsider.com/metaphors-for-nature/

Matthew, Philip. *Finding Leo*. Wipf & Stock, 2021.

Mealtrain. https://www.mealtrain.com/

Merriam-Webster.com Dictionary, s.v. "civility," accessed March 12, 2025. https://www.merriam-webster.com/dictionary/civility.

Merriam-Webster.com Dictionary, s.v. "curative," accessed March 11, 2025. https://www.merriam-webster.com/dictionary/curative

Merriam-Webster.com Dictionary, s.v. "excellent," accessed March 12, 2025. https://www.merriam-webster.com/dictionary/excellent.

Merriam-Webster.com Dictionary, s.v. "honesty," accessed March 12, 2025. https://www.merriam-webster.com/dictionary/honesty.

Merriam-Webster.com Dictionary, s.v. "humility," accessed March 13, 2025. https://www.merriam-webster.com/dictionary/humility.

Merriam-Webster.com Dictionary, s.v. "lie," accessed March 12, 2025. https://www.merriam-webster.com/dictionary/lie.

Merriam-Webster.com Dictionary, s.v. "patient," accessed March 12, 2025. https://www.merriam-webster.com/dictionary/patient.

Merriam-Webster.com Dictionary, s.v. "training," accessed March 13, 2025. https://www.merriam-webster.com/dictionary/training.

Merriam-Webster.com Dictionary, s.v. "work ethic," accessed March 12, 2025. https://www.merriam-webster.com/dictionary/work%20ethic.

National Geographic. "Birds That Fly in a V Formation Use an Amazing Trick." January 15, 2014. https://www.nationalgeographic.com/science/article/birds-that-fly-in-a-v-formation-use-an-amazing-trick

Ronald Reagan Presidential Library and Museum. "Jelly Belly* Jelly Beans and Ronald Reagan." Access date March 13, 2025. https://www.reaganlibrary.gov/reagans/ronald-reagan/jelly-bellyr-jelly-beans-and-ronald-reagan

Shaw, Douglas. *The Six Essentials of Rapidly Growing Nonprofits.* Douglas Shaw & Associates, 2022.

Statistics Canada. "Labour Force Information Analysis." December 2009. https://www150.statcan.gc.ca/n1/pub/71-001-x/2009012/part-partie1-eng.htm

Statistics Canada. "The Daily-Labour Force Survey, April 2020." Released May 8, 2020. https://www150.statcan.gc.ca/n1/daily-quotidien/200508/dq200508a-eng.htm

Stewart, Hillary. *Cedar.* Douglas & McIntyre, Vancouver/Toronto and University of Washington Press, 1984.

Sturtevant, William T. *The Artful Journey, Cultivating and Soliciting the Major Gift.* Institutions Press, 2004.

The Literature Network. "Hope is the Thing with Feathers." https://www.online-literature.com/dickinson/827/

U.S. Bureau of Labor and Statistics. "Great Recession, Great Recovery? Trends from the Current Population Survey." April 2018. https://www.bls.gov/opub/mlr/2018/article/great-recession-great-recovery.htm

U.S. Bureau of Labor and Statistics. "Unemployment rises in 2020, as the country battles the Covid-19 pandemic." June 2021. https://www.bls.gov/opub/mlr/2021/article/unemployment-rises-in-2020-as-the-country-battles-the-covid-19-pandemic.htm

U.S. Climate Data. "Climate Forks – Washington." Access March 17, 2025. https://www.usclimatedata.com/climate/forks/washington/united-states/uswa0149

Williams, David B. *Homewaters, A Human and Natural History of Puget Sound.* University of Washington Press, 2022.

ABOUT THE AUTHOR:

DOUGLAS K. SHAW

Douglas K. Shaw has been the Chairman/CEO of Douglas Shaw & Associates, a leading direct response fundraising firm, for 31 years. During his 45-year career, he has consulted with hundreds of high-impact leaders and companies. His firm raises hundreds of millions of dollars annually for nonprofit organizations and ministries that change the lives of men, women, and children.

Doug holds a Bachelor of Arts degree in History from Simpson University and a Master of Arts degree in Theology from Fuller Seminary. He is the author of three other books: *The Rules of Fundraising*, *More Rules of Fundraising*, and *The Six Essentials of Rapidly Growing Nonprofits*. Doug resides in his home state of Washington, where he and his wife Kathryn enjoy entertaining family and friends while exploring the wonders of creation.

DON'T MISS THESE OTHER BOOKS BY DOUGLAS SHAW

THE RULES OF FUNDRAISING

The Rules of Fundraising is an authoritative guide for nonprofits. There are inviolate rules for successful fundraising, but they've never been written down, until now. Not following them will likely lead you to a much longer learning curve, and quite possibly failure.

MORE RULES OF FUNDRAISING

More Rules of Fundraising—a continuation of *The Rules of Fundraising*—provides 35 additional rules, never before written down, that must be used in order to be a success in your fundraising efforts.

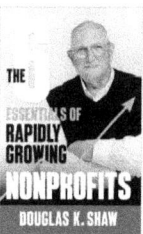

THE SIX ESSENTIALS OF RAPIDLY GROWING NONPROFITS

What are the common traits all rapidly growing nonprofits share? *The Six Essentials of Rapidly Growing Nonprofits* holds the answers to this oft-asked question! A must read for everyone who serves by working in a nonprofit organization, including board members, CEOs, and Development Officers.

241

www.ingramcontent.com/pod-product-compliance
Lightning Source LLC
Chambersburg PA
CBHW071347210326
41597CB00015B/1569